Love Stories

Inside Stories of an Outdoor Girl

Love Stories

Inside Stories of an Outdoor Girl

Shannon Tyree

Dedications

Tom,
Tap. tap. tap

****

Mom,
Thank you for teaching me to read, which made me love stories
and story telling.
Thank you for letting me try and fail, try and wipe out,
try and get up, and try and succeed.
Thank you for not bubble wrapping me.
Thank you for understanding my need to go and do.

Table of Contents

Chapter 1 - Confession of a Love Affair 1

Chapter 2 - Fishing License 9

Chapter 3 - The Stick 13

Chapter 4 - Compass 21

Chapter 5 - "Hunt it Up!" 25

Chapter 6 - Suburban Girl ...35

Chapter 7 - Men in Black 41

Chapter 8 - Decoy 49

Chapter 9 - Horse and Hunt 55

Chapter 10 - Orvis, Stormy, and Bean 61

Chapter 11 - Hit and Run 65

Chapter 12 - Opener 69

Chapter 13 - League Night 77

Chapter 14 - Camo 89

Chapter 15 - Fish Out of Water 95

Chapter 16 - Knife Flight 103

Chapter 17 - Jimmy Choos and Aunt Flo 109

Chapter 18 - Easy to Moderate 117

Chapter 19 - Shark Week 125

Chapter 20 - Snowflake 133

Chapter 21 - Don't Get Me Wrong 139

Chapter 22 - Girl Group 151

Chapter 23 - 23andMe, JB and BigFoot 159

Chapter 24 - Miss Muffet 165

Chapter 25 - Damn Visor 169

Chapter 26 - Supermoon 179

Chapter 27 - On In Two 191

Chapter 28 - Defeat Heat 199

Chapter 29 - Wonder Bread 207

Chapter 30 - That Bastard 215

Chapter 31 - Scorching Texas 223

Confession of a Love Affair

I had a love affair. We met once a week during the summer for six years. It started innocently enough. You know, with a guy from work casually asking me if I was interested in getting together for some fun. He said he'd heard I was pretty good and wanted to see for himself. So, we went out on a Saturday, arriving and leaving separately.

I guess I impressed him, because he asked if I would like to get together every week. I justified it by convincing myself the practice would do me good and agreed. Oh sure, I knew the consequences. Once word got out, I'd get a reputation. But I just couldn't stop myself because I loved it so much, and it made me feel so good.

There were usually four men at a time with me. All of varying skill levels and each with different equipment.

So here it is, the sordid details of a typical weekday evening rendezvous. Forgive me.

******

Pop…pop…pop. Driving down the gravel road into the gun club I could hear the familiar sound of shooting from trap teams that had arrived earlier than ours. I rolled my windows up, not to shut out the shotgun blasts, but to keep the road dust from getting into my car.

Easing my 4Runner into a parking spot, the gravel snapped and sputtered under my wheels. Thursday was my favorite night of the week, and I was eager to grab my gear and get to the clubhouse.

Pop…pop…pop. The shooting continued as I opened the back door and snagged my gun case. I pulled out my shotgun, grabbed my vest and two boxes of shells. After shutting the door with my foot, I headed into the evening.

I was the captain of our team. Not a big honor, mostly it involved writing our team name on the sign-in whiteboard when all of our guys had arrived, getting us in the queue to shoot. Nonetheless, I was proud of my position. It was a sign of my team's confidence in me and in my remarkable penmanship.

I leaned Winnie, my 12-gauge Winchester Model 12 with the slightly bent barrel, against the large wooden gun rack in my favorite spot. I'd set her within one of two particular spaces each week.

No different from sitting in the same pew at church every Sunday. Was it superstition? Not sure. I only know that it worked.

I threw my shooting vest on the picnic table and placed my boxes of shotgun shells on top. Then I looked around to see if any of my teammates were there.

Inside, I made my way to the bar to pay five bucks for my little blue trap ticket, which I would hand to the trap boy before shooting. Nodding to a few of the guys I recognized, Mike the bartender came over to take my money and ask me how my week was. Great guy, good bartender, and the best trapshooter in Minnesota. No kidding — state champ.

When all our team members had arrived, I did what they'd elected me to do — I wrote our team name on the board near the screen door entrance. Two pen colors to choose from, blue and red. I always chose red because it seemed appropriate. We were The Love Covenant, after all.

I loved the guys on my team. I loved being outdoors on a beautiful evening shooting, and I loved that they were self-confident enough to go along with that name. Especially when I drew little red hearts after it like some 16-year-old girl writing her boyfriend's name in the margins of her school notebook.

Let's be clear, The Love Covenant was one of the tamer names, considering the guys from Gang Bang shot the same night. That was also the team whose lowest scoring shooter had to wear a pair of ladies pink panties on his head the rest of the evening. Clearly, they had their own method of low-scoring aversion tactics.

The gun club had been at that location since 1969, and for many years it was in the middle of nowhere. Now development had crowded around it, but it still managed to survive. Thrive, in fact.

The clubhouse and picnic tables are located atop a small hill, and the five trapshooting ranges are below. It is a stunning setting, and as we shot over cattails at the edge of a pond surrounded by oak trees, it was easy to forget we were inside the city limits.

Once a trap range opened up, we'd grab our guns and head down to shoot. But first I would stop at the whiteboard and draw a line through our name. With the blue pen, of course. Down the gentle hill to another wood rack, much smaller, where we'd rest our guns while getting our shells out and putting in our earplugs. The trap boy would collect our tickets, and we'd walk out to the appropriate distance. Earlier, someone from our team would have checked the standings, posted on the wall next to the bar, and also learned what distance we were shooting from that evening.

I'm not sure how we ever really decided where everyone would start from, as there are five shooting positions. I guess it sort of just happened. Except for one of the guys on our team. He was like a robot, always starting from the center, or third, station. He shot with the same movements every single time. He stood motionless. He loaded his gun the same way. He said, "Pull" the same way, fired the same way, and rested his arms the same way. Maybe that's why he was always one of the best scorers on our team.

I, on the other hand, was all over the place. I tried different things: keeping both eyes open, one eye shut, seating the gun in different spots on my shoulder. All five of us had different styles.

The actual trapshooting took only about 15 minutes. But we were always there for the entire evening.

Once we finished shooting, it was back up to the clubhouse, guns on the rack. Someone would head inside for a cheap pitcher of beer while the rest of us would find a spot at our picnic table to review our scores, make excuses, and begin the ribbing.

The picnic table is where the evening truly began. Endless topics of the day were discussed and heartily debated: sports, movies, pop culture, cars, sex, religion, politics, you name it. We spent the night laughing and carrying on about everything under the sun.

We also spent a lot of time talking about serious matters, but I have never laughed harder than some of those nights listening to everyone's frank and animated stories about growing up, embarrassments, triumphs, and their goofy families. One time, around the Fourth of July, the Robot told a story about growing up and his crazy neighbor who set off fireworks as if he were Ted Kaczynski. We laughed so hard we wiped away tears for the next ten minutes. I still chuckle to myself when I think of that night. I loved those guys.

Sometimes after the league shooting was done, a couple of us would head back down to a range and take turns shooting doubles or wobbles, or we'd shoot someone else's gun. But mostly we just time spent at the picnic table with each other.

One Thursday night it was my birthday, and Mike the bartender, allaround good guy and best shooter in the state said, "Happy birthday" and held his gun out to me. He wanted me to shoot it. I was stunned. This wasn't any old Winchester Model 12 with a slightly bent barrel. This was a custom-made, $25,000 trap gun he had recently acquired. In front of all my guys, I graciously turned him down. Believe me, I wanted to shoot it.

But I just couldn't allow my chi to rub off on it. Not that I'm superstitious or anything, but what if I jinxed him? I think some of my guys were disappointed, but they eventually understood. It was Mike's incredible gesture that left an impression with me. Have I mentioned how much I loved those guys?

The Robot had a mint-condition, restored '71 GTO. It was gold and gorgeous. Of course, he never drove it to the range, what with the gravel driveway and parking lot, but we'd spent a fair amount of time talking about that car, our first cars, cars we'd owned, and those we wished we'd owned.

The Saturday following my birthday, Tom and I were outside in the front yard when I heard a roar coming down our quiet, tree-lined street.

It was the cherry GTO. The Robot got out, threw me the keys, and climbed in the passenger side.

He was not going to let me say no to his gesture. I looked at Tom, who pointed at the driver's side open door and said, "Go on."

I got in and nervously turned the key. She purred. After the drive, I couldn't thank the Robot enough. It meant everything to me and reinforced how much I loved those guys.

That night at dinner I looked up from my plate and, more than a little choked up, told Tom that if I died, I wanted my trap team, The Love Covenant, to carry my coffin. Not in black suits, but in their jeans and shooting vests with a box of Federal 8-shot target loads on top. He nodded and handed me his napkin to wipe my eyes. He totally understood that I loved those guys.

Most Thursdays we'd close the place down. No one was in a rush to get home. The sun would set over the cattails, and the popping sounds would fade. Gradually the picnic tables and gun rack would empty, and the trail of dust would settle as the shooters' trucks left us behind. Some evenings Mike would close up the clubhouse and tell us to just, "Lock the gate when you leave." Only when we couldn't take the mosquitos anymore did we head out too.

Years and years passed with every hot summer Thursday night the same: show up, sign up, shoot it up, and drink up. We laughed, told stories, and laughed some more. We showed up for each other. It was perfect. But just like everything in life, change crept in. One of our guys moved, another became a dad and couldn't make it every week. But the real change occurred after the wives showed up.

I'm not even sure how it happened, but one night towards the end of the season it was decided that the wives would come and we'd grill out after shooting. Have a picnic of sorts. In two words: buzz kill. And just like any affair, it wasn't long after the wives found out that we didn't shoot anymore. Oh sure, we finished the season, but the next year when I sent out the notice...crickets.

At the time I was devastated — crushed really. No matter how it ended, I look back on those summer nights with such fondness and feel so fortunate to own those memories. They made me better, shooting made me better, life at the picnic table made me better. Even if it was just knowing I had something fun to look forward to that made the rest of the week better.

Not long after that, a friend who knows me well, and knew how disappointed I was, suggested I read a book called *Bowling Alone: The Collapse and Revival of American Community* by Robert Putnam.

In it, the author describes why our behavior has changed and that we have become increasingly disconnected from one another, revealing how our social structures have disintegrated. It's an interesting sociological study that required 544 pages to explain why we aren't a nation of teams and leagues anymore. As a jilted lover, I can tell you in one word: wives.

Fishing License

It was April. We drove together, just him and me. We never really talked a lot in the car. Mostly we listened to the radio. We'd been to this place a million times before. His boat needed a new battery, and it was time to get our annual fishing licenses. The sports store in town was a favorite place to knock around and look at new gear. My dad was a gear junky; I'm proud to say I take after him.

We arrived, and he soon found a clerk who could help him with the battery for his Boston Whaler. I certainly don't know anything about marine batteries, so I just browsed around looking at the latest and greatest in fishing tackle, all the while watching my dad deal with the clerk.

Let's just talk about his Boston Whaler for a moment. If you're like most Minnesotans lucky enough to have a boat, it's probably going to be a Lund or an Alumacraft. This was especially true back in the 70's and 80's. I guess the high-end guys were buying Rangers or something. Nice boats if you like things that glitter. Anyway, I grew up with a dad who always had Whalers. Awesome boats, just not very Minnesotan.

Anyway, we got to the checkout, and he told the cashier we needed fishing licenses. My dad paid for everything, and the cashier gave us our licenses. And like every single time for the past 50 years, he folded his up and tucked it into his wallet. Choking back tears, I slid my sunglasses off the top of my head and down over my eyes; I couldn't let him see me crying. This was supposed to be just a regular outing. Only it wasn't. This was the last trip to that store he'd ever make. We both knew it.

I couldn't help thinking about the optimism he showed. He'd been through radiation and chemotherapy. Nothing was working. But buying that fishing license was like saying everything's normal. *Hey, I'm going to make it.*

On the way home, like on the way there, we didn't talk. Same as always, but somehow different. I was scared by the uncertainty of his future. We sat at the stoplight, each of us staring straight ahead.

I thought about how he'd taught me to fish, how to be quiet in the woods, and how to shoot guns. All the things he loved to do.

He was a sharpshooter and competed in tournaments. He recorded everything — the wind direction and speed, the grains in the ammo. Every tiny detail catalogued in a little notebook he kept in his breast pocket.

How many times had we gone to the range before the opener? My job was to watch through the spotting scope, telling him where he'd hit. Same place every time — center target. His hunting buddies had given him the moniker One Shot. A perfect name, since that's what he always said we got in life — one shot, one chance.

When I was little I'd watch as he packed up his big green Duluth Pack. It would all be staged in the dining room for days before he left, and then he'd be gone for a week. My mom would tease him, and he'd tell her, "Jan, if Southdale Mall was only open for a week, you'd be pretty excited too." A week or so later, I'd get home from school and there'd be a deer hanging in our garage.

On summer Saturdays when I was a little kid, my mom would wake me up really early and he and I would drive out to Lake Minnetonka. My dad always took me along, probably to give my mom some relief. She'd pack us bologna sandwiches and Hershey's milk chocolate bars. Sometimes we'd even stop for a shake at Burger King on the way home, if I was good.

We fished into the late afternoon and hardly ever talked because he said it would scare the fish, and I believed him. Now I realize it was a way to stop me from going a mile a minute.

We'd fish then drive to a new spot, fish some more, and drive to a new spot. He knew that lake like the back of his hand.

He died while I held that hand in late August.

Later that fall, a dear friend of mine who'd known my dad for a long time asked if I wanted to fish in a bass tournament on Minnetonka with him. I said yes, of course. We didn't talk much, because, you know… I'd probably scare the fish. We'd fish then drive to a new spot, fish some more, and drive to a new spot. He knew that lake like the back of his hand. We won that tournament. In fact, we killed at that tournament. Not in a Whaler, but in a boat that glittered.

The Stick

"A little to your left," I said then motioned with my finger. "Okay now a little higher. We have lots of pillows, remember?" Tom fastened the screws in place, and we hung the stick on the wall behind our bed in our new house. Ah, now it felt like home.

That stick is not merely a decoration or piece of art, but a symbol of who we are as a couple, accompanying us to every new house. Here's why...

"Yuck," I told Tom, "fish guts." We were in the fish cleaning shack at a camp on the Pipestone/Jackfish chain of lakes in Ontario, Canada. Like a surgeon, Tom was filleting our day's limit of walleyes. The large wood cutting board was carved up pretty badly from years of sharp knives — a good sign as far as I was concerned. I played with the hose, squirting spiderwebs in the corners of the stinky, old wooden shed and generally added nothing to the filleting task at hand.

Thumb pressed on the end of the hose, I'd moved to the corner of the steps, trying to remove fish scales that clung like mollusks to the old boards. Out of the corner of my eye, I noticed a group of men unloading their gear and the day's catch from a couple of beat-up Alumacraft boats with the word "RENTAL" stenciled in red spray paint on the sides.

"Y'all have a good day?" asked one of the men on the dock, looking at Tom. Whoa, Nelly! This guy is *not* from here. I thought this could be fun and threw the hose down. I went over to the dock for a closer look-see.

Tom glanced up from his patient, smiled, and said, "We oughta be having a pretty good fish fry tonight."

I inspected their catch and yelled out to Tom, "Come here!"

"In a minute," he said without lifting his head.

"Oh, man, you *have* to see this!"

That got his attention. Well that, and I gave him a look that might make you think they had Nessie in their boat.

The sound of the boats bobbing and clanking against the dock faded the moment they pulled the stringer up from the clear water. It took two of them to lift it all the way out. My jaw dropped, and just then a man stepped out of the second boat, his hand extended.

"Young lady, I'm Charlie."

I'm sure I must have introduced myself, but I was stunned and the only thing I remember managing to say was "Holy cow!"

Tom wiped his hands, ducked his head on the way out of the shack, and came to the dock. Charlie introduced himself and "the boys."

Never have we seen a stringer that heavy before. My head swirled. First of all, these "boys" were from the South, and I don't mean just south of Canada. I mean way south. What did they know about fishing Canadian waters? Second, rental boats — really? And last, people actually go out actively fishing for northerns? Nonsense! I was in a state of total confusion.

"Y'all trust me, ya hear," he said.

Huh? I thought, not letting on that he might as well have been speaking a foreign language. He was friendly, and I was soon charmed by the crusty old fisherman from Tennessee.

"Trust me, them's the biggest damn nothuns, hidin' in that lake, and if y'all don't catch one in the first cast, I'll eat my hat."

Well, after hearing that and more tales later that evening about how unbelievable the fishing was where they'd spent the day, we were hooked.

The campfire snapped and crackled, and by the light of the Coleman lantern on the picnic table, Charlie and Tom talked and looked at maps, marking ours with all kinds of notes. I was excited until I learned their fishing hole was in a lake that had no boat landing and no road access, so we'd have to carry in everything needed to fish them "nothuns."

It meant we had to portage. Merriam-Webster defines "portage" as the "carrying of boats or goods overland from one body of water to another around an obstacle." Apparently neither Merriam nor Webster ever portaged anything in their lives, because if they had, they would have more precisely defined it as "to endure torture" or "to test your physical limits against your common sense."

Because there were no motors on the resort's rental boats, we'd have to take our 9.9 HP Evinrude outboard, which I used to consider small, at least compared to the main motor. But then, I had never carried it for over a quarter mile down to a lake and back again.

We also took a slimmed down version of Tom's tackle box. "Why are we taking so much stuff?" I asked, looking at the big box.

"Because, Shannon, we don't' know what we're going to get into, and I want to be prepared."

Seemed logical, but it also seemed like more than I wanted to carry. We had four fishing rods to carry too. I've managed to break a tip off walking out of my garage. Now I had to dodge a million trees? Great.

In addition to the things that will help you catch a fish, we had water, life jackets, regular jackets, a three-gallon gas can, toilet paper, and a couple of Slim Jim's. After all, we were going to be there all day.

We crossed our lake in the early morning. The sun was just waking up, and it was chilly enough to see your breath.

Our boat raced across the water, underscoring its stillness. Approaching the opposite shore, Tom eased off the throttle and our wake soon caught up with us and rocked us gently forward with one last push. Tom stepped out and pulled our boat up onto land, tossing the anchor into the weeds. I began hauling out everything we needed.

Tom took the trolling motor off the boat, and we stood there looking at the pile, wishing we had a magic carpet. He headed into the woods.

16

"Where are you going?" I asked.

"I'm looking for a stick. We need something to hang all this stuff on so we can make it in one trip."

I've always said that before couples get married they should be required to hang blinds together or to wallpaper a room to test their

compatibility and foul language tolerance. I know now that I could add portage to that list.

I surveyed the pile of stuff again and began adding up the weight and yelled to him, "Better make it big one."

He came back with a sturdy cedar limb that looked like it had been lying on the forest floor for a while. The stick was about 88 inches long and tapers from a diameter of eight inches in the middle to about five inches near the ends and finally to jagged points. It was as soft and smooth as velvet and had one long, beautiful twist in it.

We did our best to load everything on the stick: the motor, the gas can, and the tackle box first, followed by the life jackets, regular jackets, and the toilet paper roll — just barely fitting on the end. We'd each have to carry our rods in one hand.

The smoothness of the stick was in stark contrast to the footpath. Of course, it was a rocky, watch-your-step, tree-dodging, branch-snapping, mucky trail. It was a gear-swinging two-step that had to be carefully choreographed because we were connected by the 88 inches of that stick.

Too bad Arthur Murray offers no lessons for this dance through the woods. It was slow going, because of our nine-inch height difference, the weight we carried, and the way everything swayed with each step. I could never keep a comfortable position, and I focused on not snapping the tips of the rods I carried. The longer we walked, the farther it seemed. Everything doubled in weight.

"Only a few hundred more yards," Tom said, shifting the stick's weight over to his other shoulder.

"Oh God, are you kidding me?" I said, frustrated and breathing hard, barely able to take another step. Always the cheerleader, he added, "You can do it. Just change shoulders if you need to."

I yelled at the top of my lungs, "This damn fish better be worth it!"

This was a make-your-own-way, push-through-the-brush kind of deal. My eyes went from fixed on the ground, making sure I had a safe place to step, then up quickly to make sure the rods were okay. My shoulders were sore, and my mouth was running. "Why are we doing this? I thought we were walleye fishermen. Do we even like eating northerns? You know, we're going to have to make the same trip back."

Silence from the front of the stick. Looking back on this now, I realize the man's a saint.

Finally, we made it down to the shore. In unison, we hoisted the stick off our shoulders. I collapsed on the ground, lying on my back, spread-eagled. Tom looked at me like maybe I was being a little too dramatic. We could see where the rental boats were waiting. Charlie's two boats were tied up, and it looked like they'd left some of their gear for their trip back this afternoon. *Smart idea*, I thought.

Tom went to look at the other rentals to see which would best fit our needs. I remained on the sandy shore, looking skyward and already thinking about the trip back.

After a quick inspection, he picked one and said, "Come and help me tip this over, we need to get rid of the water inside."

With a heavy sigh I pulled myself upright, dusted the sand off my butt, and walked over. The bottoms of the boats were filled with leaves and rusty rainwater that smelled like it had been there for a while. Spiderwebs ran from the bows to the seats.

They all looked pretty much the same. I don't know what made him pick this particular boat. I helped him turn it over, and when it was back upright, I checked it closely for spiders.

We unhooked everything from the stick and sorted it, then Tom attached the motor to the back of the boat. I leaned our prize possession against a nearby tree. We loaded everything up and got as comfortable as we could. After the hot and sweaty portage, it felt good to sit down.

We sat in quiet isolation, and I watched Tom rig our lines. The only sound was the water lapping on the shore rhythmically, like a slow metronome. Then I said, "Remember Charlie saying that we'd catch a big northern on the first cast or he'd eat his hat?"

We chuckled about all the energy we'd already put into this, but all good things require a little effort, right?

After a few pulls on the Evinrude, we backed off from shore and started on our way. With the map open, Tom guided us out along the point Charlie had described. I opened the bail, and with my index finger holding the line, I reached way back, then flung it forward and let my finger off the line, casting a country mile. Splash.That night we all had fried northern for dinner and no hats.

Twenty-eight years later that stick hangs on the wall behind our bed as a reminder of that walk we took through the woods early in our marriage and the journey we've been on since. Now we just need to hang the blinds.

Compass

I stopped, turned around, and realized I was confused. Confused not only because I was lost for a moment, but because I was not *used* to being lost in the woods. Panic had not set in, but I could see him stepping up to the porch to ring the bell.

I was sweating and searched for something familiar. Only nothing looked familiar. *Where am I?* How could I recognize anything when all I saw on the way into the woods were my feet and the ass end of a moose evaporating right before my eyes?

I was in completely unfamiliar territory, both literally and figuratively. While chasing the moose, I had been looking down half the time, ensuring my footing was good and protecting my expensive camera. *Damn, I lost them. Now what?*

****

We were driving leisurely south along the Kenai Peninsula in Alaska, taking in all the beautiful sights for the first time, when a moose cow and calf crossed the road.

"Holy cow, pull over, Tom!"

I'd never seen moose before, so Tom immediately drove onto the side of the road. I fumbled for my camera and lens but soon leaped out of the rental car and tore off into the woods after them. I heard, "Shannon, wait," but I was already on the chase and didn't stick around to hear the last part of the sentence.

I tried to keep my eyes on her, and followed for as long as I could. But I never managed to get the shot. I accepted that I wasn't going to get the picture and, disappointed, I turned around to head back to the car and realized I'd become completely disoriented. I'd gone in much, much farther than I realized (I *really* wanted that photo). It all ended well of course, but only after I heard Tom's familiar voice yelling, "Shannon" did I have any sense of where I was.

I've spent so much time in the woods that I took for granted my ability to navigate. However, my little foray into the Alaskan wilderness after momma moose drove home two things: I shouldn't be so cocky.

That, and I should work to improve my photography skills. How do the paparazzi do it?

The first time I remember being lost or separated and scared for real was when I was about five years old. My mom had brought me shopping in Target, and one minute we were together and the next we were not. I looked around and couldn't find her. Panic was not only at my doorstep, he was inside, making himself at home. I was next to the jewelry counter, and since my mom was not shopping for jewelry, we can only assume some glittery object had called to me.

I was alone, and my mom was gone. Tears flowed, and then some nice lady with her own kid knelt down and asked me if I was lost and where my mommy was. But I'd been taught not to talk to strangers. More confusion set in: I needed her help, but I wasn't supposed to talk to her. Luckily, before I had a complete meltdown, I heard my mom's familiar voice calling, "Shanny?"

Of course, I didn't have a compass with me either time, but even when I do I don't always trust it. I think sometimes we toss aside our better judgement and allow our instincts to take over. Why is that? Our eyes mislead us; we misjudge space and time, and it gets us into trouble, à la Alaska.

Tom and I have an agreement that if we get separated, we go back to the last place we were together. This has come into play several times, since both of us seem to be attracted to shiny objects and are easily distracted. The first time we hunted together, I got all my scent-free, camouflage clothing on and right before we walked out the door, Tom pinned a little fish-eye compass on my camo shirt with instructions to check it frequently and *always* trust it.

I never go hunting without it. It's cute and looks like a little ball. I pin it to my left breast pocket and frequently look down at it as I make my way through the woods. I feel confident wearing it. When I see interesting landmarks, like scrapes or rubs, I glance down at my compass, then around like I'm setting a marker or something. It seems to work.

The area where I used to do most of my hunting is familiar to me now. So while the compass is there, I don't need it. It's more of a back-up. The landforms and tree masses are all markers. However, now we are hunting in a totally new forest. We moved to Arizona and are learning the lay of the land. So I'm back to looking at that compass frequently as I walk into my hunting spots.

In a way it's a metaphor for life. At first you rely on help — others to lead you, or a tool, like a compass. Soon after you become comfortable and rely on your instincts and your experience. I'm in new territory now, literally and figuratively, and a compass has come in handy.

Shiny moose, sparkly jewelry, or a new place to roam. I don't know, maybe I need to curb my impulsive nature, trust my compass, and never feel lost again.

Hunt It Up

"Hunt it up," I said as gently as I could then tossed the duck wing about a foot ahead of my Nova Scotia duck tolling retriever puppy on the living room carpet. I got just the reaction I hoped for.

Bounding over to it, he lowered his head, picked it up in his mouth, then looked over at me.

"What, this? Is this all you want? Is this all you want me to do? Put the duck wing into my mouth? Easy cheesy! I got this!"

Then with several steps of his paws, he did what I had imagined and invested in him to do. Bounding back, he dropped it from his soft mouth onto my lap.

"Good boy, good boy," I said, using my best lovey, positive-reinforcement voice. Playfully roughing up the fur on his neck and loving him up, I was filled with pride and a little bit of relief. He was nine weeks and one day old. Training had begun.

As he grew, so did the duck wing distance. A puppy who would grow to be only 35 or so pounds, he was still really small, like a fluffy stuffed animal, something Steiff would make. His little legs and eager attitude carried him tirelessly. I sent the wing a little farther each time. Soon, I had it tied to a tennis ball so I could really toss it out there. Of course, we were now outside and no longer retrieving in the living room. We'd go to the park nearly every day, since duck season was only about six months away. I wanted to make sure he was ready. I wanted to make sure *I* was ready.

Tom was definitely ready and had been preparing for this since the last duck hunting season, saving the wings from the mallards he shot. The day before we left for the breeder's house to pick up our new puppy, Tom took the box of wings off the shelf in the garage. Using duck wings is a great way to train a soft-mouthed duck dog. The dog learns the smell and the texture. So far, so good.

We named him Rip after his father, Harbourlight's Riptide. Waiting for his birth should have given us plenty of time to think of a name, but when we went to pick him up, we didn't have any particular names in mind. At least nothing we could agree upon. After seeing his father, Riptide, we didn't have to think about it at all. They were identical. They had the same markings and the same demeanor.

Rip's retrieving was rock solid, whether it was in the park, in the yard, in the house, anywhere. If a sock or something fell out of the laundry basket between the dryer and the master bedroom, sure enough, my little shadow scooped it up in his mouth. Then when I noticed, he'd drop it on the carpeting at my feet, expecting a "Good dog!" and more loving up.

Retrieving on land was one thing, but soon we'd need to get wet. I was excited and a little trepidatious about our first water retrieve, hoping he'd be as successful as he was on dry ground. I told Tom, "Those little webbed feet better be all they're hyped up to be."

One warm summer evening after the dinner dishes were finished, we headed out to the lake. One couple, one puppy, a duck wing, and a bunch of old towels. There was lots of excitement leaving the house. Rip always knew when he was going with us. He had no idea what we had in mind; he just knew he was along for the ride. That dog had to be right in the mix all the time, sitting up, looking ahead, and watching out the windshield as if he were navigating.

We chose a weeknight, hoping the beach wouldn't be too crowded. There were only a few kids still playing around in the water; most of the beach was empty. Tom grabbed the duck wing from the truck, and Rip knew good times were in store for him. Half walking and half jumping, Rip didn't take his eyes off Tom and the wing in his hand. I could practically hear him: *Oh boy, it's the wing! Fun things happen with the wing!*

After tossing the wing on the beach a few times, Tom and I waded into the water up to our knees, deeper than Rip was tall. He didn't follow. Instead, he reached the water and stopped. *Uh-oh,* I thought. Saying in sugary tones, "Good boy, Rip, good boy," we motioned for him to join us. Tom flashed the wing. We could see he was excited because he wanted that wing so bad, his tail wagged and his whole back end went with it. But we could also tell he was agitated because the clear lake water lapped at his paws, and this was new and scary. An older couple watched from a bench nearby. I could tell they were rooting for the little golden fluff of a pup. They were smiling at the sight of Rip earning his water wings.

Rip, meanwhile, would look down at the water, its gentle waves reaching for his paws. A few times he put his nose down to smell it only to have the wave fill his snout. It was moving, and he was learning. Separated by ten feet or so, we gave him every indication that things were okay. We stayed in the water, encouraging and talking to him.

Sure enough, after a few minutes of pacing and sniffing at the edge of the water, he finally couldn't stand being left alone, and in a literal leap of faith, he bounded in to us. Another milestone. He was in.

"Good dog, Rip!" I cheered with a huge dose of pride added to my regular positive-reinforcement tone. I heard clapping and looked up to see the women applauding and the man gave us the thumbs-up signal.

"Hunt it up, Rip, hunt it up," Tom commanded and tossed the wing just a little ahead of the direction Rip was already paddling. We were still in pretty shallow water, but there was no need to worry.

Once it was close he lunged for it, grabbed it, turned around, and swam back to Tom, delivering the wing.

We didn't want to wear him out, and we wanted to leave him wanting more. So, after retrieving in the water for about five minutes, Tom and I headed back to shore. That doesn't sound like a long time, but in terms of a puppy's attention span, it's plenty.

We motioned for Rip to come while we sloshed back to the sand, where, for the first time, he shook the water from his coat. The first of a million lake water shakes. You know the one, it starts with the head and neck, and pretty soon the dog's entire body is shaking right down to the tip of his tail.

"Good dog!" I said. "Good dog!"

He sat down and looked up at me. His tail, like a wiper blade on high, was making a fan-shaped indentation in the sand. His look was of intense focus, almost as if he were saying, *C'mon, Shannon, just throw it one more time! Please, please, please! C'mon, one more toss!* So of course, I threw the wing, over and over, but I stayed on the shore.

He'd run into the water like David Hasselhoff on *Baywatch*, swimming out to rescue that mallard wing. Then, with the same intensity, he'd run up onto the beach and drop it at my feet. Or Tom's feet, depending on who'd thrown it. Every time there was much rejoicing and positive reinforcement. Then a big shake, followed by staring one of us down until we threw it again.

About a half hour later, it was time to go. One happy couple, one happy puppy, and a pickup truck smelling like wet dog. Training was on target.

After the beach training, we could all feel it: the beginnings of a deep attachment. My fuzzy golden-haired puppy and I were bonding. Tom and Rip were connecting too. The dog trusted us, and we knew that he would be, well, reliable. He understood, even at that young age, that we were now a pack, and each of us had a role. Rip was the official retriever of all things thrown, tossed, or dropped. It's an important position and just what we wanted from him.

In return for this valuable skill, we took care of his needs — the finest kibble, top quality veterinary care, and a custom memory-foam dog bed with his name embroidered in script lettering. Above all, he was loved and respected as a member of the family, a member of the pack.

One of the best feelings a hunter can have is the realization that the puppy you hoped would be birdie, turns out to be. I've known people who bought dogs after doing their breed and breeder research in order to find their special hunting buddy.

Then, unfortunately, it turns out the dog isn't suited. Either scared of the water, scared of the gun blast, or just uninterested in the hunt. Never really comprehending his or her role in the hunting pair relationship. Sad really. Still great pets, but that bond between hunter and furry assistant just doesn't pan out.

Rip's next hurdle? It was time to shoot over him. No delaying it. This was the true test. It's great that he'll bring back a wing, but those wings are going to be attached to a body. That body is going to be ready to retrieve only after pretty loud sounds, coming at random times. "Hunt it up" will take on a much bigger meaning.

The night before we left for the woods, I opened up our shotgun cases on the dining room floor. The smell of gunpowder combined with a little Hoppe's No. 9 cleaning solution is unmistakable to a human nose, let alone a dog's more powerful sniffer. He nosed around seemingly uninterested in the whole thing. Whenever he went near the cases, he earned a "Good dog" from me.

The next morning when we were ready to go we got him excited about the trip. Not hard to do now, since all you needed to say was the word "car." Then he'd run from wherever you were to the kitchen door that led to the garage. He was going to show you in case you'd forgotten where the truck was.

The drive up north to our place in the woods is about an hour and a half. The whole time Rip watched out the windshield. At first lots of houses and cars. Then fewer houses and more trees, then fewer cars. Eventually, only big trees to see. It wasn't his first time up there, but this time we were on a mission.

When we arrived, I unloaded the truck while Tom pulled out his Old Town canoe. He dusted out a few cobwebs, stepped in, sat down, and patted his knee, saying, "Come" in a tone that meant "right now." It's tough when the side of the canoe is just a little shorter than you are. But Rip stood up, put his front paws on the gunwale, then hopped in.

We sometimes hunted ducks on a large bog, and other times we floated down a little stream with lots of twists and turns. Plenty of areas for ducks to hide.

Rip would have to get used to jumping in and out of the canoe, as well as settling down and riding in it while we floated or paddled.

This was one of the benefits of having an eventual 35 pound Toller, compared to a 70-pound Lab. After playing in the canoe for a while and getting him comfortable with that, it was time to go shoot.

We left the canoe out and headed into the woods with our shotguns and shells. One couple, two 12-gauge shotguns, and one happy-to-be-along dog.

We stopped in a clearing, and I told Tom, "Why don't you take the first shot?"

Rip was standing between us with a check cord attached to his collar and my foot on the other end. Tom thought having a 30-foot rope to catch would be a good idea, since running after a scared dog was not my idea of fun. Tom was not shooting at anything, just firing to see Rip's reaction. He loaded his gun, then looked at me like "Here goes," which I had already interpreted to mean "This could decide the entire future of our bird hunting." Tom squeezed the trigger. *Bang!* Nothing. I looked at Rip, who looked at Tom and then me.

The only change was that he'd been sitting and was now on all fours. Tom fired again. *Bang!* Still nothing. Nothing was exactly what we'd been hoping for. Not a care in the world that two shotgun blasts had just gone off twenty feet from his ears. I unhooked the check cord from Rip's collar and tossed it aside. Now it was time to have him associate the blast with a bird retrieve.

Tom would shoot the gun, I'd throw the tennis ball with the wing attached to it, and yell, "Hunt it up!" Time after time, Rip would run after the wing and bring it back to us. Training was going really well.

Soon, the warm summer days cooled off into the best time of the year — autumn. The beautiful colors of fall leaves meant duck season. No more training. Rip was ready.

We got up before the sun and drove out to our favorite place on the bog. One excited couple, one trained puppy, and a whole lot of confidence. We paddled out to our spot, where the canoe sort of rests on top of the bog. Rip hopped out and sniffed around.

Tollers are not meant to stay at your side in the blind or canoe like Labs or other duck dogs. "Tolling" literally means to lure or to flirt. They do not scare the birds overhead, since their behavior mimics a fox's.

It was a perfect duck day, gray and overcast. This meant low-flying birds. We waited, while Rip played around us. We waited some more. Rip would come to the canoe, and I'd love him up, scratch his ears, and send him on his way. He could walk atop the bog with no problem. Hunting is a lot of waiting, a lot of patience. Duck hunting is no exception, but at least with duck hunting you can talk to your hunting buddies. You don't need to sit in silence like bow hunting deer, for instance. I don't remember what we were talking about when Tom, eyes cast upward said, "Shannon, eleven o'clock," meaning where in the sky I could find the birds.

Giving a pretty good lead, I took a shot at about one o'clock. I hit the first of the three big mallards. I yelled to Rip, "Hunt it up," pointing as the bird splashed down. This was it, this was the moment the entire past year was about.

One shot, one moment in time when your dog, for the first time, swims out to retrieve your bird, not just a wing.

And just like that, three little words, "hunt it up," made one couple grateful for a golden-haired pup, who brought the bird to my hand and looked up at me as if to say, *"That's it? That's all you wanted me to do? Easy cheesy! I got this!"*

Suburban Girl

Not long ago, I was crossing the street from my parking ramp to my office building in downtown. It was Monday, so I was careful to dodge the spot on the sidewalk where someone had thrown up, likely on Saturday night. That same Saturday night I was in the woods.

As the loud, stinky bus accelerated by me while I waited on the street corner, I thought, *Somehow I need to make the change from a suburban girl who works in the city and longs for the outdoors to an outdoor girl who occasionally visits the city and checks in with friends and relatives in the suburbs.*

For instance, no matter where I am I'm always paying attention to where the sun is, and which direction the wind is blowing. Saturday was especially windy. It was late afternoon, and Tom and I had decided to head out to one of my stands. I would sit, and he would take a walk, carefully and quietly around me making a big, wide circle.

Approaching the area where my tree stand is located, Tom pointed out a couple of fresh looking scrapes. Some buck had been there recently. I got very excited thinking I might see a big buck, Grandpa, as we call 'em. At the bottom of the stand, Tom held my equipment as I climbed the ladder. The old wooden stand is wobbly for sure, not creaky, just a little shaky.

With the gusty wind, the stand and the soft white pine it's cozied up to were swaying like lovers on a dance floor. Warily, I looked down at him, and he gave me the it's-okay-just-get-up-there look. I reached the top, but with nothing to grab on to for leverage and wearing enough clothes to resemble Bip the Michelin Man, I wasn't particularly nimble. I had no way to get up on the platform. Exasperated, I climbed back down, still swaying, and was met by Tom's disappointed look.

Since we have an unwritten rule about not talking at our stand sites, no words were spoken. I stood for a moment, took a deep breath, and reassembled my determination, conviction, and my camo bib overalls that had ridden up a bit during my futile climb. After waiting for the wind to die down, and getting a reassuring nod, I started my ascent.

Only to once more get stuck at the top, where there was still nothing to grab. With no Cirque du Soleil training, I was forced back down the steps, this time with the weight of shame and humiliation pulling me towards the ground. Now what? Why couldn't I get up there this time?

Precious time ticked away. I gave him a desperate I'm-sorry-what-do-I do-now? look. He handed me my bow, went up the steps, retrieved the five-gallon bucket I sit on, and searched for the best ground option.

Okay, I thought. *It won't be that bad. And if I do get any chances at Grandpa, just imagine the excellent angle I'll have!* Or so I told myself.

Tom set me up in an area 15 or so yards from my swaying stand, in a spot where I'd be out of the way of the scrapes, able to see down into the meadow, and still be hidden enough to prevent my profile from showing. Comfortable on the ground, I gave him an enthusiastic thumbs-up sign, which this time stood for "I'm sorry I'm not a monkey nimble enough to climb into that stand today, but I appreciate you making this accommodation for me. I'll be just fine!" I was all adjusted and feeling confident in the embrace of a young white pine. Let the games begin.

Gust of wind...nothing. Gust of wind...nothing. Big, big gust of wind...nothing. For close to an hour I looked across the meadow into the setting sun, where the blonde grass waved back and forth and rippled hypnotically with each gust. I watched it start from my left and blow across to the right. The noise from the oak leaves seemed delayed from where I was watching the wind, until it reached me.

Dry, brittle oak leaves dangled and shook like go-go dancers, making a loud rustling sound.

The sun had just dipped below the tree line across the meadow at the top of the hill, and the wind died down. That's when I heard them — slow, heavy-sounding paw steps. I was paralyzed. Sitting there on my bucket about two feet off the ground, I realized how much safer and more confident I felt in my tree stand. Up there, nothing really ever saw me or could smell me easily.

Suddenly, I found myself questioning the success of the recent bear hunt. How had that gone? Had I heard anything about that? Seen any pictures in the local paper about it?

Any sense of being cold was long gone, replaced by a warm, flushed sensation. I tried listening as carefully as I could, trying to discriminate between those damn oak leaves rustling and the paw steps. I was listening so hard it was like I couldn't hear anything, like my ears just turned off. Listening "so hard" means I'm squeezing my eyes shut and fussing with the settings on my hearing aids. I wonder why we close our eyes to hear better?

I opened my eyes to see the sun really going down now, and while everything has turned to a beautiful, monochromatic, rich sepia color, I begin to freak out about my senses becoming limited. Everything was happening too fast. The sky was darker, the wind picked up, and something behind and downwind of me was walking about.

Do not focus on bears. Do not think of bears. All I could think about was bears. Do I run? Do I just sit still? Do I start thrashing around and hollering for Tom? What does the officially adopted hunting manual say about this situation?

Just as I'd convinced myself that I was bear chow, three does bounded past me from left to right. My head snapped, and I was jolted by how close they were and how low I was. They sprinted as if they'd seen something that frightened them.

Breathing more heavily, I concentrated. On what, I don't know. Suddenly it felt very dark. When did that happen? I wished Tom would come and rescue this suburban girl from heavy paw sounds.

No such luck. I was left there to sit in the dark to listen and wait and wonder what was going on around me.

See, the steps sounded sloshy. I know, I know, and let me just say that I realize "sloshy" is probably not a word my dad ever used to describe steps he'd heard to his hunting buddies. They sounded heavy, careless, as if it didn't matter who heard.

There I sat on my bucket, going through the Audubon book of mammals in my head, with the only criteria being: what doesn't care if it's heard? Hmmm… that might be a new category for the Audubon Society.

Without warning, I saw the best thing I could have hoped for: Tom walking up from the meadow in front of me. He moved quietly, without saying anything, and seeing him was like it always was, surprising and a relief for a suburban girl. Even one who wishes she could stay in the outdoors forever regardless of how scary it can sometimes be.

Men in Black

Looking back from my seat in the front pew, I wondered who those men were sitting together in the last row. I paid attention to the service, but I kept looking back at them hoping something would trigger my memory. They were all wearing dark suits and had the same general appearance, but who were they? I kept thinking I would recognize them. But I didn't.

Our church was quiet and still, intensifying the emptiness I felt inside. I watched through swollen eyes as smoke from the incense rose in a perfect coil up to heaven, or at least as far as the choir rafters. The priest finished speaking knowingly about his parishioner of 34 years then gave his blessing. Everyone got up slowly and shuffled out.

Except for me, sitting and staring ahead at the large crucifix hanging behind the altar, wondering what I was going to do now without my dad. When I finally did get up, the men in the back pew were gone.

It's been many years, but I still can't get them out of my mind. Who were they? No one in my family knew either. I did know they weren't his coworkers, they weren't neighbors or friends, or hunting buddies. Without an answer, my wild imagination has filled in the blanks about those men in black.

When I was just a little kid, maybe five years old, my dad, a very quiet man, handsome and fit, a nonsmoking, non-drinking, tough, disciplined, dependable former Air Force guy, worked for a giant computer firm. Way back when big giant computer companies were uncommon. He traveled all over the world for them. Doing what? I don't know (cue the theme from *Mission Impossible)*

We lived minutes from an international airport. All I know is that regularly we'd all pile in the aqua blue Jeep Wagoneer, sometimes still in our feeted jammies, and drop him off. "Bye, Daddy, I love you." He'd be gone for weeks, and then we'd go back again, sometimes in our pajamas, to pick him up.

In those days, back in the late 60's and early 70's, you could still walk to the gate and wait. The plane would pull up, and soon a line of strangers would begin passing us, making the anticipation grow. Then finally, the moment he'd appear at the door of the jetway. "Daddy!" we'd yell, rushing him like a rock star. Then lots of hugging.

I feel sorry for anyone who didn't get to experience that type of gate arrival.

Waiting near the luggage carousel, he would unzip his baby-blue and white TWA bag and pull out a little treasure for me — a little doll or trinket representative of where he'd been. I'm sure he bought them in the airport gift shop on the way home. But what had he been doing on those trips? And were those men part of it?

I can remember the mailman at the front door handing me the day's mail. In the stack would be correspondence written on thin, crinkly paper marked "Air Mail," addressed to my dad, Delano.

"Who's Delano, Mommy?" I asked the first time I saw that because, to me he was Dad, though I knew other people called him Bob. My mom explained that my dad's name was Delano Robert, and official things came addressed that way. "Mommy, what's official?" I can only imagine the line of questioning I gave her over the years.

I also remember getting picture postcards from St. Petersburg, Russia, from a man I knew as "Uncle Eric."

Only we weren't related (*Mission Impossible* theme, anyone?). I thought he was so neat, and on the rare occasion he visited our house he would call me luv. Did he know those men, and would they call me luv?

Sometimes after eating dinner and watching Walter Cronkite, we would head downstairs to his workbench. On the shelf to the right was a radio, and he tuned in stations from all over the world. We listened as he worked reloading ammunition. A competitive sharpshooter, he reloaded his own ammunition to make it *just* the way he wanted.

He would sit me to his left on a red wooden stool near the end of the bench and say lovingly but firmly, "Be still." So I sat there trying not to wiggle and watched.

Occasionally I'd get to fill something. I made sure not to spill. "Thanks, Daddy. Did I do it right?" I'd ask, searching for an attagirl.

"Yes, babe, thank you," he would say and then ask me something like, "Do you know what time it is in London? How about Stockholm?"

Of course I knew where those places were, because together we would look at an atlas and talk about where he was going. But mostly I just sat quietly and watched him putter. Occasionally he'd chuckle to himself about something he heard in another language on the radio. He would look at me and smile.

"Was it funny, Daddy?" I'd ask.

"Yes, babe." he'd answer, continuing with his project. It was a very large black radio, bigger than a bread box, with huge dials.

I couldn't understand what was being said, unless it was the BBC. Were they listening and chuckling too? Those men in black?

When he was finished reloading, he would tune in the world clock on the radio. It always sounded so ominous, and if I heard it today I bet it would still seem kind of spooky. There'd be a sound like a metronome, and then, near the top of each minute, a man's eerie voice would come on and say, "At the sound of the tone, the official world time is..."

He would announce the exact time, and then it would go back to ticking. My dad would set his Omega watch, turn the radio off, and say to me, "Look at the time, off to bed with you, young lady."

Why would he be setting his watch to a precise time? Did those men know why, and were they also setting their watches?

Often on the weekends he was home, he'd drive us in his Wagoneer out to the gun range. After telling me to behave and to sit still, he'd put giant earmuffs on me and set me up next to him. My job was to look through the scope and tell him where he hit. Dead center every time. Sometimes there would only be one hole after many shots. He was so methodical. Everything was just so. Were they as particular?

He shot a variety of weaponry at varying distances, and the farthest he would shoot was 500 yards. When you're six or seven that seems like a really long way. Heck, even now it seems like a really long way; it's probably a par five. At the range he kept track of everything, writing details down in little spiral notebooks: the time of day, the wind direction and speed, the temperature and humidity, and the grains used in the ammo. His sunglasses were not to be touched, ever. He was meticulous in his details. Were the men at his funeral that exacting?

Along with *Field & Stream* and *Outdoor Life*, the mailman would deliver *Shotgun News* and *Soldier of Fortune* magazines. My dad was an avid and successful outdoorsman, hunting and fishing during his time off. He met the same deer hunting buddies for years and years. The ones who had given him the nickname One Shot were at his funeral. Did any of them know those men?

In addition to the complete and well-stocked gun vaults, he was a collector of knives. In particular, I recall were Randall Made Knives. Big, beautiful knives. The curve of the blades and the carved handles are exquisite.

To accompany the knives, he had sheaths that could be tied to your leg or other parts of your body, concealing their beautiful, but dangerous, potential.

He was expert at sharpening his knives, and when I was a little older we'd sit at the kitchen table, where he'd show me how to do it properly using oil and a stone while sharpening his fillet knife or his bowie knife that he used hunting. I practiced on steak knives. "Nice and easy, babe. Try doing it in one easy motion," he'd say. I wonder if their knives were as sharp?

He was a prepper long before that became popular, and I knew that if anything happened, our family was going to eat, drink, medicate, and be able to defend ourselves with no problems. I knew what a go bag was long before that term became part of the popular lexicon. Were they prepping too?

But then, gradually, he did less and less international travel, until it stopped completely. Soon after that, we stopped reloading, and he stopped shooting as often, except to sight in his rifle for deer hunting season. We didn't listen to the world radio, and we didn't set our watches to the world clock anymore. He wore a Rolex now.

No more airmail arrived and no more postcards from my Uncle Eric. In fact, no more Uncle Eric. Where was he? Did those men know? (Theme from *Mission Impossible* fades away.)

When he died, he left this mystery behind, and a few questions. Later, when my mom was cleaning out the basement, behind boxes and boxes of freeze-dried food packets, she found a box of my dad's pictures and mementos. It was like a treasure chest. Sifting through it, we tried figuring out who was in those black-and-white photos with the pretty scalloped edges.

At the very bottom of the box I came across an essay my dad wrote in high school back in 1954. As I sat down on the old red stool, I could hear my dad telling me not to wiggle. I got comfortable and began reading the handwritten pages. Apparently, the assignment was to describe what you wanted to be when you grew up. Now, many years later, he was gone, and I was reading the imaginative story of a 17-year-old with his whole life in front of him. The boy from a tiny town in Missouri wanted to work for the national Forest Service as a ranger. Making sure my tears didn't fall on the tender yellowed pages, I imagined right along with him what it would be like working for them. Walking through the woods together, side by side, working as rangers, me and my dad.

Reading his words, I envisioned him wearing one of those green uniforms and the brimmed hat, standing in front of a stream near the mountains. He looked good in a hat. I had seen where life had taken him. It was not to any National Forest, but rather to the suburbs. Instead of wearing the cool uniform in a natural environment he wore a suit every day to the big giant computer company.

After breakfast, I would stand on the couch and help him tie his tie. "You look good, Daddy," I'd say, proud of my knot. He'd tell me, "Thanks, babe," while making a few adjustments. Then I'd watch from the picture window as he'd go off to work in the completely man-made world of supercomputers.

Soldier of Fortune? Computer analyst? Spy? Dad? Maybe the question isn't who were those men in black, but rather, who was my dad?

Decoy

I was back at home in my comfortable rocker out on my front porch. It was a perfect Minnesota Sunday evening, around 68 degrees. I'd just finished cleaning out all the turkey hunting gear and equipment from my SUV. For fun, I'd stuck one of the decoys in the front yard near the street. Since we lived in a neighborhood full of walkers and bikers, it was sure to draw some attention. I rocked and wondered how many neighbors I'd pull in with the decoy.

None so far, but my dog, Rip, was curious. His tail was tucked between his legs as he slowly approached the fake bird. But soon it was nothing more than something to sniff at.

Uninterested, he walked over to me, nudged my knee with his cool, wet nose, circled a few times, and then lay down. I watched as his eyelids grew too heavy to stay open. The endless parade of walkers, kids with training wheels, and owners being walked by their dogs passed by. They tried not to stare at the obvious and out of place turkey decoy.

Soft fluff or "cotton" from the trees slowly drifted through the air and accumulated along our driveway, right where it met the lawn, like some kind of late-spring snow. As the cotton floated lazily across my view, I automatically assessed which way the wind blew.

My thoughts transported me to a place far beyond the suburban front porch, to a familiar place deep in my mind. A place that reaches up to my consciousness whenever I watch and feel the wind blow: my deer stand.

My guess is that most of you hunters experience this to some degree. For instance, you're in your car at a stoplight when you notice the car dealership's flags blowing sharply in one direction. You no longer see the blue Chevy in front of you, instead you're looking at your favorite hunting spot. You're daydreaming, remembering a particular hunting situation, when suddenly...*HONK!* Jolting you right out of your camo is the agitated lady in the silver minivan behind you with her hand on the horn.

Hunting is so peaceful.

****

Ah, finally. My neighbor Bill, who lived kitty-corner across the street, couldn't ignore the decoy. Proudly, I thought, *I knew the decoy would work.* As soon as he reacted to the decoy I yelled out, "Yep, it worked!"

Rip got up slowly, wagged his tail, and greeted Bill in the driveway as if he were in on the joke and had gone to retrieve him.

Bill chuckled, realizing what had just happened. "Nice one. You got me!" he said, laughing like he'd fallen for something he's too smart to have fallen for. "How was the hunt?" he asked and sat down to rock with me.

"It rained the entire time," I told him, adding, "The rain made it hard to concentrate, and I wasn't sure they'd be off their roost."

Starting Friday, our first day hunting, it rained enough to consider looking up the Do-It-Yourselfers Guide to Ark Building plans. It felt like duck season rather than turkey season. But you can't let a little (or in this case, a lot) of rain get you down. Persistence! As it turns out, that was the tenth rainiest May in recorded history. Just our luck.

"How do you know any birds were even around?" he asked as he petted Rip's ears.

"The night before, I blew a crow call then waited and listened for them to respond," I explained. "They did, so we knew they were in the area." Bill's not a hunter but was interested to understand how you go about finding turkeys. We chatted some more about the weekend and how the rain had stopped, of course, on Sunday afternoon when it was time to leave up north and head home.

"Well, I'm sorry you didn't get anything," he said, getting up. Bill had listened long enough to hear my tale of woe. About how it was hard to hear anything gobbling back to us with the rain hitting the leaves, the wind howling, and the whip-poor-wills singing their incessant song — *whip-poor-will, whip-poor-will, whip-poor-will* — and on and on and on. "God's alarm clock," I always say.

"Have a good night, we'll see ya later," I said.

He gave Rip a final pat on the head, walked off the porch, and waved to Tom in the yard.

Turkey licenses are distributed by lottery. We'd felt fortunate just to draw permits. However, we'd felt a little unlucky drawing the last days of the spring hunt. By that time, the leaves are all out, the birds have been shot at by five weeks' worth of hunters, and finally, they may need a little Viagra — I think they might have lost a little of that lovin' feeling. Still, we were very excited. Once you turkey hunt, it stays with you. Every time I go I think about how it's my favorite hunting experience because it's so challenging. I swear they have a sixth sense. My dad always told me, "If they could smell you, you'd never get one."

Tom loves it as much as I do and is always patient with me. He's determined to be my hunting and fishing guide. I think he feels bad when I don't bring something home. I watched him cutting the lawn, maneuvering the Lawn-Boy around the decoy, and I thought about how much of a guide he really is for me, whether hunting or in day-to-day life.

The decoy next snared Pat, who lived next door to Bill. I waved at Tom and flashed "two" with my fingers. He smiled, nodded, and kept on mowing. As soon as Pat neared the decoy, I yelled over the noise from the mower, "Well, that's two now!" and "It's working!"

Pat laughed, scratched Rip's, head and told me how he'd skipped work and gone fishing. "We limited out on walleyes," he said, trying not to sound like he was bragging. He'd fished a lake not too far from the cities, a place known for its walleyes.

"Good for you, man!" I said, sharing his elation. I'm genuinely happy for anyone limiting out on walleye. It had been a while since I'd caught my limit, and our opener on the Whitefish Chain was not pretty.

"How'd ya do this weekend, with all this weather?" he asked, sounding like he already knew the answer.

"I didn't see a dang thing," I told him, sounding more down about it than I had intended. But I really wasn't happy about it. I love to turkey hunt, and it can be difficult the best of times, let alone with all the miserable rain.

"Well, maybe next time," he said. Then he chuckled and told me, "At least we know the decoys work!" He got up to go tuck his kids in for the night.

"Yeah, good night, Pat."

He walked down the driveway with Rip's escort, right arm up to acknowledge Tom, who made a diamond pattern in the lawn with the mower. Tom nodded and continued.

I rocked in my chair, dog by my side. There were still a few big clouds in the sky, but it had now turned into a soft, peachy-lavender dusk. The smooth rocking motion relaxed me, and I imagined the sun being pulled lower in the sky by an invisible string. The whine of the mower faded a bit, as Tom had gone around the corner of the house. My neighbors Doug and Gloria, who lived directly across the street, arrived home from their lake place, where they went almost every weekend after the snow had gone. As they pulled into the driveway, they looked with mild curiosity at the decoy, but with no real surprise.

We'd lived in the neighborhood long enough by then. They didn't seem taken aback or alarmed by much of what we did anymore.

They finished unpacking their car, and Gloria waved to Tom, who was finished mowing and pulling the mower up the driveway.

"What's that in your yard?" she asked.

Tom yelled back, "It's a neighbor decoy."

Smiling, she said, "Well, it's working." And with that she disappeared into her house. Soon after, the garage door slowly closed.

The sky has turned a pretty shade of deep royal blue. Trees were in silhouette. The sun had set on another hunting weekend. Rip and I walked down, I removed the decoy from the yard and put it in the box marked TURKEY on the garage shelf.

Tom and I took a moment on the porch in our rocking chairs and looked around at the pure white cotton that had accumulated all around us.

"Thanks for mowing the lawn," I said, acknowledging his efforts.

"Your little neighbor decoy experiment worked."

"Yeah," I said, feeling very content, "it sure did."

"Sorry we got skunked, babe," he said and put his hand on mine. I looked over at him, smiled, and thought, *somewhere tonight there's a gobbler flying up to its roost*. Well, that and *Geez, where did all this cotton come from?*

Horse and Hunt

"A hundred and two point three? It can't be. I have to go hunting today," I told my doc while sitting on the exam table in field pants and boots.

"The thermometer don't lie, kid," he said and asked where we were going hunting. I continued to pinch the cotton ball between my thumb and fingertip, where earlier Nurse Janet had pricked it.

A little too eagerly, I might add. She'd grabbed my index finger, and I jerked it away saying, "Whoa, not my trigger finger" and gave her my middle finger…ahem.

"My company has a membership at the Horse and Hunt Club," I told him. He just nodded while listening to my lungs.

I'm sure as a hunter and lover of the outdoors, I have the best doctor in the world. I knew I'd like the guy the minute I walked into his tiny waiting room and instead of *Good Housekeeping* and *Redbook*, the messy coffee table was filled with *Guns & Ammo*, *Field & Stream*, and *Shotgun News*. Oh yeah, a few *Highlights* were scattered around for the kids.

"Well," I asked, "Can you fix me up? I have to be at the club to take my clients out in an hour."

The look I got was priceless.

He told me as a medical doctor sworn to uphold the Hippocratic Oath to go home and rest, take a couple of aspirin to kill the fever, and drink plenty of fluids to stay hydrated. The hunter in him told me to have fun. "If they fly, they die."

He was in the middle of a story about his hunting dog when Nurse Janet returned with the bad news — my white blood cells were sky-high. Before walking out of the room, she looked over at me and said, "You look terrible."

"Thanks," I said, letting all the air escape from the latex glove I was blowing up. Doc pulled out his 'scrip pad and told me antibiotics for the next five days. Followed by, "Have fun" and he could use a little pheasant meat. "If you know what I mean…"

Note to self: Remember to drop off a couple of pheasants for Doc.

I swung by the drive-thru pharmacy, gave them my prescription, and was on my way. No backing out for me. I was sweating, and the temperature outside was in the 30's. It had been pretty cold the night before, and there was a thin coat of ice on the shallow ponds.

After arriving and seeing where my guys were, I parked and opened up my SUV, getting all my gear out. I filled my pockets with Kleenex and aspirin. I had several layers on both the top and the bottom, and I wanted to strip right there, I was so hot. Pretty soon we were all assembled and ready, standing around talking. The guide from Horse and Hunt came over, told us which field we were going to start on, and how each was stocked: a bunch of pheasants, chukars, and one turkey.

"Sounds like fun," I said. "Let's go!" Trying to rev myself up. Guys and guns and dogs and gear. Away we went.

We walked toward our first field. My body ached, and my nose was running. We lined up along the edge of the field. There were four of us, and I took the far-right side. I was sweating and out of breath already.

My sunglasses were fogging up, and I wanted to take my knit cap off but knew better.

One of the reasons I bought Nelli, my Benelli Montefeltro 12-gauge shotgun, was because she was so light. I thought she'd make a great field gun, one that you could carry all day. Today though, it felt like I was lugging around a Spanish galleon cannon.

Our rental hunting dogs had been bouncing around like Tigger, but before I knew it they were in front of me — frozen.

I wasn't used to hunting with pointers, but they were beautiful dogs, so athletic, and made bird hunting fun. I kicked up the birds, shot and missed both roosters. I got "the look" from my hunting buddy next to me and a few teasing jabs were thrown my way. I deserved them.

"Focus, Shannon," I said under my breath.

Again, we started walking. The dogs were sniffing and going nuts ahead of us. My buddy was talking to me about how nice it was to be outside and not back at the office in front of a computer when...*crack!* My right foot went through the ice up to my calf and into this low swampy area that had barely frozen over. "Oh my God," I said under my breath, hoping no one heard me.

"What's going on?" he asked.

I just shrugged and with a fake smile said, "Oh nothing, nothing."

We still had a lot of the field to go, and a couple more after that. We weren't even close to being finished. I tried reminding myself that it was a gorgeous day, blue sky and just a little breeze. But all I could feel was the sweat running down my back and my right foot soaking wet, squishy, and cold.

Pretty soon we had dogs in front of us again, looking like furry statues. *Pop! Pop!* went my gun. Got 'em! Leaning over to pick them up I felt dizzy. Dizzy, but happy — two roosters.

It would have been a really long day if I was skunked. Stuffing them into the back of my vest, I thought, *here you go, Doc!*

We eventually finished our fields and managed to shoot all our birds, including the turkeys. I turned my birds in and headed to the bar. As I reached for the 7-Up I'd ordered to wash down more aspirin, the bartender asked, "Uh… are you feeling okay?" He gave me that look a guy will give you when he doesn't want to tell you your hair is bad and maybe you should check your makeup. I swallowed my aspirin, threw a couple of bucks on the bar, and went downstairs to the ladies room.

"Terrible" would have been an understatement. "Oh dear God" again, hoping no one could hear me. My hair was soaking wet where my cap had been and was sort of frozen on the ends, in an icicle, crunchy way. My face was a ghostly white with red, clown-like cheeks from being outside for the past four hours. Steam rose up from my neck, fogging the mirror as I leaned in for a closer inspection. There was no trace of the "24-hour, waterproof" makeup I'd put on eight hours earlier. It had melted off long ago. Nice.

Without anything to tie my hair back, no makeup to fool even the casual observer, and no women around for a little sisterly help, I figured, what the hell? I took a paper towel, patted myself as dry as I could and went back to the bar.

The rest of the evening was a blur. We had a few drinks, told tales about our day, and ate a nice dinner. Afterwards, as we were leaving, our guide came up and handed out paper grocery bags filled with frozen birds.

I tossed two pheasants into my 4Runner and thought about how I'd just taken care of my co-pay.

Orvis, Stormy, and Bean

A friend of mine wears a Stormy Kromer hat. Every day in the cold Minnesota winter it's atop his head, keeping him and his ears toasty warm. It's awesome, and it's as authentic as he is.

"Let me take your coat and your Stormy," I said when he arrived for Friday soup night at our house in January.

"You know about Stormy?" he asked, pulling off his puffy parka. He seemed surprised.

"Of course I know about Stormy. How else is a guy going to keep his head warm and still be fashionable all winter long?" I teased then added, "I made chili."

I owe my knowledge to my dad, who would take me along shopping for hunting clothes at Gokey's in downtown Minneapolis. They were at the bottom of the Foshay Tower. A beautiful store. It's where he bought a wool hunting coat and a pair of bullhide slippers.

When I was a kid growing up in the suburbs, going downtown was a big adventure. We planned for it. It wasn't like a trip to the sporting goods stores nearby. It was a big deal. Now, when I think about it, it seems kind of ironic that we'd go the middle of a crowded city for sporting goods that he'd wear out in the middle of the woods.

My dad taught me not only about integrity in the things we bought but explained that buying quality meant your investments would last. Sure, you could buy pleather slippers, but really? Come on.

To this day when that Orvis or L.L. Bean catalog arrives, it's like time stands still for me. I stop what I'm doing and look through it page by page, savoring each item. Even though I can go to these store's websites, and I do have them bookmarked as favorites, I get a little thrill opening my mailbox to find the catalog waiting for me. Like a gift.

Is it because I'm shopping for something? No, I'm mostly just reminiscing. It feels comfortable, turning the pages, like I'm reconnecting with my dad in some small way. Dream job? I'd be working for Orvis, Stormy, or Bean. Connecting with customers who are out there, as I am, visiting those sites just because it feels good.

Recounting their stories about a special article of hunting clothing, a dog bed for their furry friend, or like me, my dad's slippers. Those bullhide slippers that he'd wear every evening after work.

"Shanny, go get my slippers," he'd say, and like a golden retriever I'd run and find them, bringing them right to him. I'd get a pat on the head or a quick hug and a "Thanks, babe." Those smooth, heavy, worn moccasins are burned into my memory.

When Tom and I were first together we took a trip out East, headed to Acadia National Park. We didn't have a lot of money, so we drove my Corolla wagon. For two days in the car, until we arrived in Freeport, Maine, all I could think about was visiting the L.L. Bean store.

"Slow down, babe. You don't want to get a ticket," Tom said from the passenger seat, looking at me as if I were possessed.

"I'm just excited, that's all." Trying to explain why I was doing 85 in a 65 mph zone.

"I don't think the trooper is going to accept being excited to visit L.L. Bean as a valid excuse," he said, still watching the speedometer.

Driving into the parking lot, my eyes were welling. I felt like a kid making the pilgrimage to Disney.

Pulling open the heavy doors to the store, I looked around. It was so much more awesome than I'd imagined.

I literally choked up and could not speak. All the products and gear I had seen a million times on the pages in the catalog had come to life. I could pick them up, try them on and even sit on them. It was magic. When is the last time anything so simple made you feel so good?

Packing for his annual deer hunting camp, my dad would use his Duluth Pack duffel. It's an enormous dark-green canvas and leather bag that will never fall apart. Now it's mine and we use it on our hunting excursions and vacations. The thing wears like iron.

When I visited the Duluth Pack store for the first time and chatted with the store manager, I couldn't wait to pass along the story of my dad's bag. He's heard a million just like it, packs handed down from generation to generation. Of course, that's why they are still in business — they create quality.

I know my life is richer because I had someone introduce me to Orvis, Stormy, and Bean. And while my dad's gone now, I'm still around to fill his shoes. Or should I say slippers?

Hit and Run

Lying on the street dead; a hit and run. Flattened except for the awkwardness of one wing sticking up. Its feathers ruffling in the breeze of the cars speeding by. I didn't see it happen, but I was at the stoplight waiting for the left-turn arrow to change, looking at the aftermath. Watching as the victim's mate paced frantically back and forth on the grass between the sidewalk and the curb. The light turned green, and I slowly made my turn, driving past the site of the fatal accident. Only no lights and sirens, no yellow body bag, no traffic-gawking slowdown. Nothing. Just its mate, trying to get as close as it could.

My tears came without warning.

I couldn't help but admire the affection it displayed. Watching that Canada Goose, I thought, *Shouldn't we all be a little envious of that amount of devotion?* Was it a female who had lost a male? Or vice versa? Were they on their way to their nest when fate intervened? What was the link that wouldn't let it leave, at least not yet? How long had they been a pair? Did they have little goslings together? There would be no obituary, no recording of its life. I wondered if anyone in the cars around me at the busy intersection thought the same thing.

This vigil — this painful, public vigil in the middle of the city — was playing out and there was no one to console that goose. The pacing made me think it was trying to somehow make sense of this. *What's happening? Please get up! We have a life to live together. Don't leave me alone. I can't remember your iTunes password!*

Its unrelenting display of grief made me see how utterly focused it was on its mate. It knew something wasn't right and acted out, looking for answers. Little black webbed feet trod back and forth, wings flapped, its head and long neck bobbed up and down. It obviously felt pain.

Hours later I drove by again, and this time the goose partner was lying down in the boulevard grass next to the curb, just a few feet away from its dead mate on the street. Weakened by grief, it had not left its partner.

The next day the surviving goose was gone. Remnants of the dead goose remained, although the wing feathers no longer were sticking up. I'm sure people who drove past it didn't even notice.

Or, if they did, were glad to see a pesky, pooping-everywhere goose gone from the planet.

But when I drove by, I couldn't get the goose left behind out of my head. When did it decide to leave? And now what? They say geese mate for life. What does that mean for the living goose? Does something instinctual kick in? And from that point on will it have to go it alone?

Once, on PBS, I saw a *Nature* program on crows. A crow had died and was lying dead on the grass. Nearby, a flock had gathered in a tree, which had become black with crows. The researchers were trying to learn if crows communally grieve the loss of another. If nothing else, did they at least acknowledge death? It sure looked that way to me. Even though they had arrived individually, the flock left together, all at once after a long period of time perched in the tree looking out onto one of their own. It was fascinating. How did they all know to come, and what was the signal telling them they had stayed the appropriate length of time?

Look, I know this goes on all over the world all the time and in much more violent ways. I'm old enough to remember watching *Mutual of Omaha's Wild Kingdom*. Cheetah? Check. Zebra? Check. Chase scene? Check. But this wasn't Mutual of Omaha in Africa.

This was a car/pedestrian accident on a street in my neighborhood, with a pair of geese. Right in front of me. Their little brains are the size of a walnut at best. Yet somewhere in there, there's something that ties the two of them together as a couple.

I hesitate to say it is love. No rings exchanged, no vows taken, just a coupling. Nature's way of keeping the species alive. Only now they have been uncoupled by a violent hit and run.

Afield, they can be a challenge. They fly high and have tough feathery chests. Getting a shot off and getting it to stick can be hard. You're usually cold, maxed out in head-to-toe camouflage, dog by your side. When I hunted them, I never had even a hint of the feeling I was experiencing now — sadness for the one left behind.

But there I was, in my car, shocked at my response when I got all misty and a few tears fell down my cheek. Was it because I imagined something like that in my own life? Did I see myself someday as the sad and confused pacing mate? *Don't leave me! This wasn't supposed to happen. I'm scared. Now what?*

I believe deep inside we're all fearful of that moment and moments like that. Of course, it seems natural because we're human, and don't like to consider things like this. When we see death in nature, on the side of the road for example, we're given a little reminder of the inevitable.

And now when I see a Canada goose, I remind myself to tell Tom my iTunes password.

Opener

Opener. I wait for it all year. Patiently. Well, sort of. The closer it gets the more antsy I become. The anticipation, whether it's fishing, duck, deer, or turkey season, is half the fun. But this time my opener was, well, eye-opening.

Some seasons the opener is about the new gear and fun new toys you might be sporting. A few years ago, it was my new compound bow. But this particular bow hunting opener, it turned out to be my vulnerability I packed.

My husband and I are great hunting buddies. Tom drops me off near my stand, makes sure I'm set, then goes on his way, returning after dark to pick me up. We've done this together for 18 years in a place he's hunted for 50 years. So, on this particular day, nothing seemed out of place, everything was right on target.

Trancelike, the only things I allowed to move were my eyes while I sat up in my stand. Not much wind. Not much sound, except a few black-capped chickadees moving from tree to tree. It was quiet on the water today too, except for the resident beaver, who, I swear, tried to hypnotize me by swimming back and forth, back and forth across the long pond.

Bow opener in Wisconsin is early enough in the year that you can wear your thin camo. No heavy overalls or coats needed. Certainly no long underwear. The sun kept me warm, even made me a bit drowsy. It had rained the day before and into the night. A good soaking rain, making the walk to my stand nearly silent, as if I were a ghost. My seat was wet, so I brushed off as much water as I could before I sat down without a lot of noise or movement. Glad I'd brought my seat pad to keep me comfortable and my butt dry. Ahh, mid-September in the woods — damp, soft, and quiet.

Sitting up perfectly straight, my left hand held my bow upright, the bottom cam resting on top of my right boot. My trigger was in my right hand, which rested on my right thigh.

70

I've thought many times that if this were a yoga pose it would be called The Hunter. I felt like a statue.

I hadn't moved in probably an hour and a half. Then, the gunshot — *bang!* — sounding like a cannon, startled me out of my Zen-like trance.

Wow! What the…? I thought. *Very close.* My stand sits high in a big oak tree near the base of a hill on one side of a little brook 25 yards from a beaver dam. On the other side, another hill covered with oaks and pines and a few birch trees near the water. The sound roared down what now seemed like an echo chamber.

Confused, I thought maybe someone was bear hunting nearby. Bears? I didn't hear any dogs, and I hadn't run across or smelled any fish piles. I'd never seen bear hunters before in this location, and it didn't sound like a shotgun either. It didn't have that "pop" sound. It was more of a harsh, sharp, bang. It was a rifle.

Hmmm, okay, sit tight.

Mr. Beaver, the hypnotist, who had entertained me while I waited for my buck, slapped his tail and dove underwater the moment he heard the gun go off. That slap, nearly as loud as the gunshot, put the entire nearby animal kingdom on notice, me included. In beaver, that tail slap clearly means something ain't right.

If I thought it had been quiet before, now it was a vacuum, a void: no sound, no movement. Only the lingering effect of Mr. Beaver's slap, its ripples racing to the pond's edges, only to be baffled by the fringe of long grass.

Uneasy, I glassed the area, looking for anything — any movement, any sign of a hunter or dogs. Nothing.

No hint of anything or anyone. So I settled back down, hoping it wasn't going to completely ruin the day's hunting.

Twenty minutes later, still no sign of Mr. Beaver. There was a tad more breeze now, and from its usual direction. I looked up to the top of my tree and into the leaves, watching them shake and wiggle, when another shot rang out — *bang!* This time it was much louder and seemed much, much closer. Without any delay or hesitation, moving on instinct alone, I hung my bow on the branch I had broken off weeks earlier. Although I was stiff from sitting motionless for hours, I was off my seat, turned, and down the steps of my tree, opting to fall the last three feet or so, in less than two minutes. Adrenaline dropped me to the ground as quick as I'd ever moved in my life. There I was, crouched down at the base of my tree. I was that scared.

There was still plenty of daylight left. Confused about what to do, I looked around. I had never talked to Tom about situations like this. Should I walk back to the drop-off point? I'm sure there wasn't a deer within a mile of my stand now between the beaver slap and the shots. Hunting was done for the day.

While still hunkered down, I covered my black hair with my camo seat pad, my ego fully exposed. Not much in the woods is that black, except bears and crows. I was scared, and all I could think about was that some bear hunter would see my black hair and shoot. I know, I know, pretty unlikely. But someone was shooting nearby. At the time I felt I was being a little foolish for my reaction, or overreaction. Or was I?

The blast had been a little too close, and I didn't know what else to do. I felt I needed to stay low and near the protective trunk of my tree. I knew I couldn't go back up to my stand because it made me feel like too much of a potential target since I was fully camouflaged. It was bow hunting opener, and I wasn't wearing any blaze orange. And because Tom drops me off, there's not even a vehicle parked nearby to hint to anyone there might be someone in the woods. I told myself over and over that everything was going to be okay.

In the midst of this I became angry too. I was mad at whoever was shooting that rifle in the woods, and moreover, I was angry at myself for feeling so vulnerable. My ankles ached in my boots from squatting, and my knees were wet from my soaking camo pants.

Motionless, I could feel my heart beat. When my ankles couldn't take it anymore, I finally sat on the ground. I watched the sun sink slowly behind the tree line, which was now a quiet navy blue trimmed with orange. No more shots were fired, but I stayed on the ground, huddled by my tree.

The sun's earlier warmth had vanished along with my adrenaline flush, and now I was cold. My senses remained on alert. I listened carefully for any clues: footsteps, branches snapping, dogs, even the forest's alarm system — crows and red squirrels. Anything. Everything was silent, and now the forest was fading into dark.

I recalled the rule that no hunter will shoot after dusk and hoped I wasn't being naive. Maybe someone had been sighting in their rifle. Doubtful. Maybe someone had been bear hunting.

I wasn't sure, and that was the biggest thing bothering me. Who was it and what were they doing? I had come up with a bunch of different scenarios while practically cowering at the base of my tree. But mostly I was embarrassed that I had been so affected by those two seemingly random shots. Two shots, twenty minutes apart and no other sounds.

Unlike most nights, tonight the darkness was my friend. I was protected by its cloaking ability. I was hidden. Usually the darkness means I start sending come-and-get-me messages via telepathy to Tom. The same messages were sent, just more urgently than usual.

I climbed back up in my tree, feeling safer up there now that it was so dark. Everything was in shades of black and blue, me included

Relief finally came when I heard the familiar sounds of Tom making his way through the woods. Shining my flashlight down on his face, I could see his big, expectant smile. Like usual, I handed him my bow and clambered down. We walked out of the woods together in silence, our footsteps quiet.

I put my gear away in its case and climbed up into the truck. Once inside, he turned to me and asked, "So, did you have a great night?"

"I got scared."

And there went his smile. Of course, he'd heard the gunshots too and knew they might trouble me. He put the key in the ignition and started her up. Then, with a deliberate motion, he turned to me and rested his left arm on the steering wheel.

In the dim glow of the dome light he looked at me for what seemed like a long time before he said anything. I could barely look him in the eye, and he waited until I did so to speak. "You have no business being in the woods if every time something like that happens it's going to upset you."

Tough words, but I understood. With that he turned around, and we drove back to the cabin in silence. We didn't talk about it the rest of the night or ever again.

That day I didn't see any deer, but I did see the light. I promised myself that no matter what, I wouldn't let this opener be any kind of closing.

League Night

"Happy thirtieth birthday!" Tom proclaimed and handed me an awkwardly wrapped $50 used Bear compound bow along with a trigger, a dozen or so aluminum arrows and a quiver. Trying to disguise a compound bow with wrapping paper was funny. Sort of like when we were kids and would wrap up the latest album to give a friend. Can't really disguise that too much, and of course every time someone would say, "Let me guess, an album?"

"Really? Wow!" I said, trying to drum up more excitement than I was feeling. I wasn't an archer, at least not yet, and had been rather hoping for something sparkly that rests on your finger. Not something you pull with your fingers. And yet, the most surprising part of the gift was still to come.

Smiling, and helping me with all that wrapping paper, he said in a very excited tone, "And…I signed you up for a fall shooting league!"

I'm sure my face still held the smile I'd forced, but was it also showing what was in my mind… *Just me, not us?*

The gift was becoming less and less attractive. "Really?" I said, trying to sound enthusiastic, not wanting to put a damper on his gift presentation. "A league? How does that work?" I said, still forcing the excitement a bit but fondling my new bow, holding it up and teasing the string back a bit.

"Well, you just show up on Wednesday nights and shoot," he said, still looking at me and the bow, sure he had done a good job with the gift. "Don't worry, I talked to the guy who manages the league. You're all set."

"So, you're not shooting? It's just me?" I asked and hooked the quiver to my jeans.

"Yep, don't worry, you'll be great."

Or that's how Tom imagined it was supposed to go.

The first Wednesday night of the league finally arrived. I loaded my black plastic bow case into the back seat. Tom gave me a kiss through the window and smiling, said, "Don't worry, you're going to be great."

Yeah, great. And I waved goodbye.

The shop wasn't more than ten minutes from my house, but since it was the first night I left myself plenty of time.

Driving around the block a few times, stalling my eventual arrival, I slowly pulled into the parking lot of King Archery, in an industrial part of town. Next door was a huge Pepsi distribution center. I'm partial to Coke and thought this was perhaps a bad omen. I parked my 4Runner next to the other SUV's and trucks in front of the nondescript gray-block warehouse building, where a little sign on the glass door let me know I was in the right place.

Of course, not knowing the protocol, and without any chance of looking cool, I stayed in the security of my car. I sat there for a few minutes trying to muster up the nerve to walk inside.

Sitting in my SUV watching Pepsi trucks pull in and out, I convinced myself that this would be a great opportunity and reminded myself that a couple of weeks before, Tom and I had gone to the local park's archery range so I could practice live firing this sucker. I needed to learn to sight in my bow for different yardages. We went a few times, so I had probably drawn back maybe 30 arrows.

Ding! — well, more like *clank!* — went the cowbell strung on the top of the door, announcing my arrival. Every head in the place turned to look at me, so apparently slithering in unnoticed was not an option. Once in, it was a tight fit. And, Jesus, what was that smell? A combination of old, moldy carpeting and burnt oil? I tried not to scrunch up my nose, but oh, man.

The entry area was so small it didn't leave a lot of room for maneuvering your four-foot bow case, let alone nine guys and nine hard-sided bow cases. Everyone was taking their coats off and getting their gear all settled, hanging their bows on large red plastic-coated hooks that were screwed into long wooden beams that went across the ceiling. I had never seen anything like it. In addition to our bows, there were ones for sale hanging all over the place, and, oh yeah, where do I put my purse?

I tried to figure out who worked there, since there was no one behind the counter. I waited.

It appeared that most of the guys knew each other, and the hushed drone of conversation was suddenly punctuated by a very friendly, "Hi, how can I help you?" directed right at me.

Bull's-eye. The already quiet room got quieter. I held my case with both hands and looked down and said, "Uh, my husband signed me up for this league. I've never shot before."

Are you kidding me? Did that just come out of my mouth? What was I thinking? That's not what I'd planned in the car on the way over, or the revision made in the parking lot. Why didn't I just come out and say I wanted to be the dorkiest person in the room?

Gerry, the owner, grinned and said, "Oh, yeah, I remember now. Glad you're here."

The next thing I knew, Gerry showed me where to hang my bow and put my case (purse inside) and told me to just "hang tight and relax" because he was going to talk to everyone since this was the first night. So, there I was just sort of uncomfortably standing in the way, trying to look like I fit in.

Looking around at my surroundings, I began to notice the guys were sort of paired off. Oh no. Paired off? I wasn't a pair. *Geez, I wish Tom were here,* I thought.

Not only did I feel like a fish out of water, now I felt like the nerdy kid picked last for a team. Well, you know, you're not really "picked" last, it's more of a resignation that you have been judged unworthy. Based on whatever was known about you or unknown, you were left standing by yourself. Then whatever side is stuck with you, decides that well, okay, we'll just have to deal with it. Except these teams were only two people.

In all my life, I've never been that kid. I've always been picked first or done the picking. This was new and awful and yet still sort of exciting at the same time.

Gerry explained what was going to happen. I listened with my head hanging down. Looking up through my bangs, I noticed a tall guy, sandy blonde hair, and pretty fit standing off by himself. He appeared almost bored waiting for the night's shooting to begin.

I think he was quickly coming to the same conclusion I was, when Gerry turned to me and said a little too enthusiastically, "Shannon, why don't you team up with Chris here?" pointing in his direction.

Smiling, I said, "Uh, sure, that's great, thanks" and nodded toward Chris, hoping to see anything resembling reassurance. None. Zip. Oh, man, what had Tom done to me? Trying for self-confidence, I kept repeating his words to me: "Don't worry, you're going to be great."

Gerry went over the night's shoot and what would be the routine for what turned out to be the three years I would shoot on autumn Wednesday nights.

He had set up five 25-yard shooting lanes, which included one tree stand up about 12 feet.

We shot into straw bales with paper photographs of a variety of animal targets, from turkeys, to whitetail deer, even javelinas.

Each of the five stations had a different position for you to shoot from, and every Wednesday they changed. For instance, station one might have you sitting in a chair that was facing the opposite direction of the target, so you'd have to twist, hold your position, then fire.

The second station, he might have had us standing on a board that was teetering on a log, so your footing was always moving until you could steady the rolling log and shoot. Sometimes he would shorten the distance in one of the lanes, and you'd shoot at 15 or so yards. There was never a time we shot at a target where we just stood straight on.

Like any new partnership, the first couple of rounds between Chris and I were awkward. He didn't say much, if anything — ever — let alone the first night. I was just glad we'd finally started shooting. Everyone was busy focusing on themselves and their equipment, and I felt a sense of relief. Of course, I let him go first as he'd shot in this league before and knew what to do. Four shots at each of the five targets.

I tried not to be stupid. I watched and mimicked what the teams around us were doing.

I didn't chat, ask a lot of questions, or do anything that might make him consider not coming back the following week.

After we'd each shot our target, we'd have to wait until all the teams were finished with theirs. We'd hang our bows on the hooks overhead, and when everyone was finished we walked up to the targets to retrieve our arrows at the same time.

They were hard to pull out of the tight straw bales, and sometimes you'd have to put your foot on the bale to pull against.

Kill shots are outlined on the targets with points, so keeping track was easy. Chris was dead-on, and I was surprised at how accurate I was once I got my 25-yard pin sighted in. As I pulled my arrows out next to Chris' I felt like, *Hey, I'm thinking I like this.*

Well, let's be honest, I like anything that I'm good at right away. Especially if there are enough people around to witness how well I performed.

When all the archers had finished the five stations, it was a quick exit. Everyone left by about 8:30 p.m. or so. Gerry hung around to sell arrows and help anyone wrench on their bow.

I went home the first night after hitting all the targets with pretty good accuracy and not upsetting Chris other than by my mere presence, and told Tom, "I think I'm going to like this."

He kissed me and said enthusiastically, "I told you you'd be great!"

Soon, Wednesdays were a favorite night of the week in the fall. I couldn't wait to get home and get my stuff together and head over. Sometimes I arrived early just to hang around and talk to Gerry. He'd usually be at his messy workbench, and I'd pull up a stool and sit and watch him tinkering away with something, but mostly I enjoyed his easy conversation and stories.

Here's a guy who retired from a career at a desk but yearned to have a little storefront where he could indulge his hobby — archery. Sure, he sold stuff, but mostly he repaired equipment, figured out tricky shooting lanes for his leagues, and helped novices like me learn more about shooting.

I was using an old used Bear bow. It wasn't fancy, for sure. But it worked. I had killed plenty of targets with it, and at the time was using hollow aluminum arrows. Carbon arrows, which is what everyone uses today, were not yet available.

As the season went on, Chris and I clicked as a team. We still hardly spoke to one another, and he still wouldn't look me in the eye. But our shooting was good.

In fact, damaging each other's arrows as a result of our prowess became a regular occurrence. Eight arrows in the kill shot on a turkey is tight, since it's a little less than the size of a quarter. We were good. Really good. Soon we were beating everyone else handily, and it felt awesome. It was especially rewarding since I felt like Chris and I were the outcasts, neither of us coming in with a buddy to shoot with.

It was for safety reasons that teams waited until all archers had finished shooting before walking up to the targets at the same time. What it meant though, was that everyone saw how others scored, and don't think for a minute they weren't keeping track. The goal of this league was to become better hunters, making accurate kill shots. Scores were secondary to the true purpose, but everyone kept score. Each Wednesday I improved and so did Chris. Together we were hot, and everyone, including Gerry, noticed. Of course he did, we kept having to buy new arrows.

For this brief time in my life, I felt so much satisfaction out of being really good at something, even if it was just shooting arrows at a target.

For one night a week, I was the best at something, and the guys I was shooting with knew it. I didn't have to say anything. "Just let your shooting tell your story," I'd say to myself.

One night up in the deer stand, Chris and I took our usual turns shooting. His first arrow went right in the heart. I shot, and my arrow went into his. The sound it made was strange.

Without saying anything, Chris shot again, and this arrow sliced open my arrow, which was already nestled in his first. It was like this huge Robin Hood moment.

When we climbed down out of the tree stand and went to retrieve our arrows, we just stood there for a moment, shocked. Seeing it up close was crazy. The other teams came over to look at it and then looked at us like we were freaks. Gerry yanked the cluster out of the bale and gave us new arrows, on the house. While we finished shooting, he grabbed a ladder and hung this trifecta of perfection over his cash register from the metal supports that held the dingy ceiling tiles.

Nobody said much. No one ever said much. But as we packed up our gear, a few of the guys nodded at me. The kind of nods that said *Good shooting* or *Nice shooting tonight* or my favorite, *Oh my God, you and Chris are the best ever!* or at least that's how I took it. But, again, the culture wasn't one of gushing, so I just sort of nodded back and looked down into my case. Smiling.

Gerry's shop was also a Department of Natural Resources big game registration station. Shooting in the fall meant that sometimes during our league night a camo'd up guy would pull in with a tagged buck in the back of his pickup. The cowbell would clank, and everything would stop.

Bows were hung up, and all of us went outside to stand in the chill and admire another archer's prize. No compliments, just questions about where he was hunting, the distance at which he'd shot it, and what kind of bow he used. That's about it. But there was an air of true appreciation around the bed of the pickup. After all, wasn't this what all of us were practicing for?

Soon though, the first season of league shooting was about over. It went so fast; we all were shooting so well.

Gerry arranged an end-of-the-year banquet at a local restaurant for all of his leagues. We had our own room. It was a little uncomfortable since this was a social event, which meant talking, and most Wednesday evenings were spent in near silence. Just the heavy snapping sounds of arrows hitting the targets. No conversation. To alleviate some of the awkwardness though, he'd hired a comedian.

He was pretty funny. Generally, I think everyone had a great night except Chris' wife. I'm not sure she was aware that her husband's partner was a woman. Oh well, that was for Chris to figure out.

The summer came and went, and I practiced at the park. Soon the league started up again, but this time I raced to the shop, meeting the bell on the door and the old-musty-carpet-and-burnt-oil smell with a smile and all the enthusiasm I could throw at them. Season two: Bring it on.

Same thing, a bunch of the same guys standing around, grouped in the familiar teams of two. And there, waiting over in the crowded corner was Chris, alone. This time however, he came up to me, and while still not looking me in the eyes, he muttered, "Hey," wanting to make sure we were partners. Ah, the difference a year makes.

Gerry had become more adventurous with his targets. We had to shoot through a tire hanging about 15 yards away, with the target behind it at 25 yards. Or he would dim the lights, replicating dawn and dusk, which, I would find out through experience, were when the bucks seem to be most active.

After the holidays he'd pick discarded Christmas trees off the curb, some still with tinsel hanging in them, for us to shoot around. He was trying to make it more interesting and difficult, and we appreciated him for that. He stepped up his efforts, and we stepped up our game.

Again, Wednesdays were a highlight of my fall. No matter what was going on in my life at home or at work, there was always Wednesday night shooting. Chris, still quiet, was shooting a new expensive bow and was now using carbon arrows. I still had my same old bow, but I too had switched to carbon arrows. Because of that, we'd never again have any Robin Hood moments.

Some things, like our equipment, evolve. Others, like Chris' quiet demeanor, stay the same. And some things, like a dormant skill, improve. It feels good to be good at something. And every time I walked through that door, hearing that bell, I looked up at our arrows sticking into each other over the cash register and heard Tom saying, "Don't worry, you're going to be great."

Camo

Camo. It makes me blend in so well that I become invisible. I have a wide assortment of camo clothing for all the seasonal changes for my outdoor life. It's amazing how many different patterns and color options there are now. Funny how I take such care dressing to camouflage myself in order to fit in to the oak savannah where I hunt, but during my normal, everyday indoor life I sometimes feel completely invisible without even trying.

I discovered this feeling alone, 15 feet up in the air in my deer stand, completely covered in Realtree® camo overalls, a coat, gloves, neck gaiter, and face mask. I'd topped it off with a rabbit fur hat, hiding my black hair. Anyway, up in the stand I have a lot of time to think, seems meditation-like, so quiet and still. I was feeling grateful for my good stand location, my excellent tree and surroundings, when all of a sudden it hit me: *I am completely invisible.* No one would pick me out. No animals will readily see me unless they come into the tree, and no one except Tom even knows I'm out here.

How invisible? I had hikers and other hunters walk right under my stand. Directly under. If I had said, "Boo!" I'm pretty sure I would have seen the most scared-out-of-their-minds people ever. Life-changing scared. Like they'd-probably-need-therapy scared. Like they-probably-would-have-experienced-their-own-personal-*Blair Witch*-moment scared. The sight of them pissed me off.

Their noise and their scent were completely ruining my chances of getting Mr. Buck that day. So I seriously considered ruining someone else's day, but because I didn't want to forever ruin this stand location, I did not. No animal would come near this tree if a couple of humans pooped their pants underneath.

Okay, I think you see the power I had being so invisible in the woods. But the revelation was that it was in stark contrast to my life out of the woods, which is sadly most of my time and where I was increasingly feeling invisible.

I'm not sure how it started. Was it when I lost my hearing? When I started gaining a few pounds and didn't want to draw attention to myself? Or was it getting older, watching the lines and wrinkles appearing on my face, like a topo map, and not feeling pretty anymore? I can't really pin it down. But it was happening for certain. I was becoming invisible. My self-esteem and my hunting camo — linked. Who knew?

I began to notice it when I was doing something ordinary, like grocery shopping. The cart is moving, but who's pushing it? It's as if people didn't even see me. Looking right past me or worse, sometimes bumping into me like I wasn't even there. So with no effort whatsoever, I am completely invisible during my regular indoor life.

But when I'm in the woods nothing bumps into me. Well usually, but that's a whole other story.

To be completely and truly camouflaged requires more than just fabric that matches your surroundings. For instance, I take exceptional care preparing for bow hunting season. A big part of that is being completely scent free. My rule for this? No perfume after Labor Day, as well as only scent-free laundry detergent, body soaps, lotions, and deodorants and definitely no garlic. Finally, I focus on being still, calming my energy, my chi, challenging myself to not move a muscle for long periods of time. Only moving my eyes, scanning my surroundings for Mr. Buck. Animals have a sixth sense that enables them to divine the ghosts in the woods. Feel things that may be near, things that might want to eat them.

So being still is a basic requirement. Many times I've had to hold my position, and breath, sometimes even after drawing back. Everything is still, nothing moving, so Mr. Buck, motionless too, will suddenly paw the ground with a front foot. Almost a stomp, very Fosse. He knows something's not quite right, but since he can't see me, can't smell me, and I'm frozen, he needs to do something to figure out what he's sensing. He's betting the stomp will tell him. Trusting his instincts and stomping the ground to get whatever it is to move. I don't. It's awesome. It's also when I let the arrow go. I want to say to him, "Mr. Buck, you were right, your sixth sense was right." But it's too late, he can't hear anymore.

Feeling invisible in my day-to-day life was happening. No stomping needed to tell me that. No pity party. Just noticed it was happening.

I realized, or maybe just finally admitted, that I sometimes camouflage my feelings as well. Masking my true feelings to blend into my surroundings, like a chameleon. Wanting to fit in, wanting to be liked, but at the same time not being exactly true to myself. An imposter really, camouflaging my real self for an opportunity to see if I could fit in. Why do I do that? Do I want to be friends with people whom I've not been straight with from the start? That seems wrong. I suspect all of us do it to some degree, concealing a part of ourselves. What if everybody is doing the same thing? The result? None of us really know who anybody truly is.

Recently, after a big move in my life, I've had an opportunity to meet a completely new set of people. I've been learning to let go of chameleon thoughts and actions. Just blending in as myself: hearing loss, weight gain, and wrinkles. Just trying to be confident again with my true colors and my stripes showing. Letting go of the imposter and learning it's not necessary to disguise my feelings all the time.

****

Walking ever so slowly, "three steps forward, two back" as Tom always says, in the woods to my deer stand, I was camo'd from head to toe. Going so slowly causes me to really absorb Mother Nature's handi-work. I couldn't get over the beautiful tan, blonde, and sepia colors that define autumn *after* the peak in Northern Wisconsin. It's strangely beau-tiful, subtle, and some may think drab. So different from the showy golds, vibrant reds, and fiery oranges of just a week or two prior.

I stopped on the narrow path, now covered in fallen leaves, just to take it in. As I stood marveling at how completely monochromatic the world seemed to be, a crow flew overhead and perched itself on a stand-ing dead oak, just to my right. A big black crow, not worried about cam-ouflage at all.

Caw! Caw! Caw! he announced loudly, jarring me out of the still-ness and breaking the precious silence like a sneeze in church. I'm sure he was broadcasting in crow that I was in the neighborhood, so watch out. Apparently seeing right through my facade.

"Thanks for nothing, Mr. Crow," I said under my breath.

But big, black, and beautiful Mr. Crow got me thinking about all those animals that don't worry about blending in. Yep, this is where I talk about bears — big black bears. Not caring in the least if they're camouflaged. Never needing to worry about blending in. What freedom! They go where they want, when they want, without a care for who sees or hears them. True liberty. No bear trying to impersonate a chameleon here. If only I could get back to that.

I too have black hair, and one day Tom came home with a rabbit-fur bomber hat for me to wear while hunting. It has ear flaps — you know the kind — think Elmer Fudd. I stuff my ponytail up under it. His con-cern was that my black hair would create a profile or silhouette. The fur-ry, multicolored hat made up of tans, grays, and browns definitely is an improvement. Other than crows and bears, neither of which are deer magnets, not much in the woods is black. Now my hair's blackness was replaced with more natural coloration, blending in. I love it, and it's become a big part of my hunting camouflage attire.

Early one morning, predawn, as the hint of the sun's rays had just begun to illuminate the still-dark forest, I woke up in my stand (I know, a bad start to a story). This happened after getting there way too early, being a little too warm and much too comfortable.

Just as I was opening my sleepy eyes, I noticed what appeared to be a giant, feathered 747 with its landing gear down heading straight for me and coming in hot.

Of course, it wasn't actually a 747, but a great horned owl. At that close range it just looked like a 747. I think it thought my hat was a real rabbit and an easy breakfast, but instead of a drive-thru it was a fly-thru. Instinctively, I threw my arms up, causing enough of a ruckus that the bird aborted the landing, allowing me to keep my hat.

After a lot of heavy breathing, a complete check of my gear, and realizing my head was still attached, I was a bit embarrassed. *Really, Shannon, sleeping?*

As a precaution, I turned the hat inside out. I didn't have any trouble staying awake after that. Readjusting myself on my seat, I thought, *It might be time to find a new hat.* One that still camouflages but doesn't scream owl chow. Lesson learned.

Like the bear and the crow, I've promised myself to be less concerned with the judgment of others and to be less of a chameleon. I've also promised to never fall asleep in my deer stand again.

94

Fish Out of Water

"They wanna race!"

And with that our crew went into overdrive, everyone taking their positions. Except for me. I turned to Pete, the boat's owner and captain, who pointed at the wheel. I'm sure I looked at him like he was nuts.

Just as I took the helm I heard the other Pete (yes, we had two Petes onboard) yell, "Shannon, you're gonna get a big puff of wind in three, two, one…"

Boom! The boat surged forward. Commands were shouted, gears were grinding. Salt spray hit us. Then, silence. Silent speed.

The sails filled, and the 52-foot Beneteau sailboat flew, cutting the sparkling azure waters of the Caribbean effortlessly. Three of the crew were hanging off the starboard side of the boat, which was now tilted at a 60 degree angle to the port side. Captain Pete was standing on the seat next to me looking up at the telltales, then to the sea ahead. I guess some people *can* see the wind.

There was no doubt the other boat wanted to race. There was plenty of wind and nothing but ocean for as far as you could see. For the next hour and a half, we raced to an imaginary finish line. The other boat signaled defeat, and just like that I was 1 and 0 in ocean racing.

America's Cup, here I come! The other boat's sailors waved and headed back. Us? We were hootin', hollerin' and high-fivin'. Reaching into one of the coolers, we passed around frigid bottles of Presidente beer to celebrate, only to find they were not screw-tops. We needed a bottle opener.

Still wearing her racing gloves, Bridget climbed down the stairs to the galley. Only a minute later she came back up with the bad news. "No opener."

This was the second day of the trip, up until then we apparently hadn't needed a bottle opener.

The first day at sea we'd been enjoying different rum concoctions, since rum is cheaper than water. And, in my mind anyway, was probably safer to drink.

Captain Pete went down the stairs, ducking his head like he's done it a million times before, and a few minutes later came back up looking befuddled. Pete had been sailing with different guests for two weeks before we arrived. Somewhere along the way the church key had gone missing.

With our race win exhilaration waning, we searched for the rum bottle to toast our victory. El Presidente would have to wait. That is until I remembered something…

****

The bottle opener conundrum really tickles me. Let me back up a little and explain why.

Earlier that year, one of the owners of the company I worked for, Pete, stopped by my office and asked if Tom and I would like to go sailing. Sounded fun, so I said, "Sure." I knew Pete had a boat on Lake Minnetonka, so I thought that would be kind of neat. I'm game for anything.

Then he said, "What I mean is do you and Tom want to go on a sailing *vacation*? I have a boat in Tortola, the British Virgin Islands."

Oh. Then I did quick geography in my head and answered, "That sounds awesome!"

Have I mentioned I've never sailed before? Should be okay. How hard can it be? It looks so relaxing.

A couple of months or so later in preparation for the week on the boat, Pete thought it would be a good idea for all of us to meet first. That kind of threw me, because up until then I thought it was going to be Pete, his girlfriend, Tom, and me.

Pete emailed everyone and gave us directions to a restaurant where he'd made reservations. I counted the number of names the email was sent to — seven. Including Pete, that meant eight on the boat. I wondered, *Just how big is this boat?*

Tom and I were the last to arrive at the Italian restaurant and were surprised when we saw we had our own little room off the main dining room. Looking at the guests, it appeared there were two couples, a single guy, and Pete. We smiled and exchanged pleasantries while hanging our coats on the back of our chairs.

A minute or so later, Pete stood, clinked his knife on his wineglass to get everyone's attention, and said, "Look around, this is going to be your crew for a week. Let's go around the table and introduce ourselves."

Which turned into "Let's all describe the sailboats we own, the racing we do on a regular basis in the summer, and what races we've done on the Great Lakes and oceans." Super.

I was seated to next to Pete, who led off, and then pointed the other direction, which meant I would go last. I quickly realized me going last would be a disappointing finish to the racing resumes and pedigrees I was hearing.

"Waitress, can I get a Pinot?" I asked, hoping a little wine would ease my spirit.

After hearing the first couple of introductions, I began to think the only way this could get more uncomfortable was if one of them turned out to be related to Dennis Conner or Larry Ellison, in which case forget about me. I'm out. One after another they vividly described different races and the conditions they've raced in: the weather, the wind, the one-in-a-million, freakish, random happenstance they overcame. The treachery, the teamwork, the equipment and gear. It all sounded so exotic. And when they spoke about their boats, it was as lovingly as someone describing their firstborn child.

What I also learned was they all knew each other. All belonging to the same yacht club and regularly sailing against each other on Minnetonka. Tom and I were the wild cards.

Where was that waitress?

But even Tom had experiences to talk about: sailing as a kid, renting catamarans when we went on a cruises in the Bahamas and during our trip to Hawaii. He'd even once been a part of Pete's crew on Minnetonka.

Tom's a big guy, six foot two and 250 pounds. Pete had asked him to be "hanging meat." Sailing slang, meaning he needed some weight because of the big winds forecasted for that particular day.

And when our neighbors asked if he wanted to buy their little 14-foot Hobie Cat catamaran, he jumped at it. Pete shared with the table that Tom had been a towboat captain and had a lot of experience on the water.

The din of the restaurant was lively, the smell of garlic was in the air, and as I listened to our new friends I wondered if my intimidation showed. Finally, the waitress arrived with my Pinot. I mouthed, "Come back soon" to her before she left. She smiled, nodded, and left.

The flames in the fireplace cast pretty shadows on the wall as we drank our wine, ate our bruschetta, and somewhere in there placed our orders. Finally, after Tom finished explaining his experience and answered a few questions about what it was like to work on the river, everyone shifted their faces, with their dreamy expressions of life on the water over to me.

Then it happened. The richly decorated, Tuscany-inspired dining room morphed into a concrete block cell. There I was, in a cheap metal chair, wrists and ankles shackled to it, and nothing but a light bulb swaying slowly back and forth overhead.

"Well," I uttered, then looked sheepishly down at the cloth napkin in my lap. "I, uh, have never been on a sailboat before."

Right there, that table of sailors, who had worked themselves into a frenzy over boats and wind and water, looked at me as if I'd just told them there was no Santa. That group, who knows the only thing better than sailing is talking about sailing with sailors who love sailing as much as they do, sat in sailing shock. Reaching for my wineglass, I shot the group a tentative smile. Where was that damn waitress?

Everything came to a screeching halt, but Pete quickly picked up on the awkwardness of the moment and said, "Let's discuss trip details, like meal planning and flight itineraries."

And just like that, I'd become sailing resume roadkill.

"Tom, I don't think this is a good idea," I said, slamming the car door shut.

"Nonsense, you're going to love this. What an opportunity," he said, and put the key in the ignition. Looking at me under the dome light, he patted my left knee and said, "You worry too much."

"Worry? How can I not worry? Where do you want me to start? Did you see those women? What are they? Size fours? And from the sound of it all they do is sail. And, what about pirates?"

"See, this is exactly what I mean, Shannon. How about focusing instead on the fact that we're going on a weeklong vacation to the

British Virgin Islands in the middle of a Minnesota winter, with experienced sailors who will be excited to share with you something they love so much."

Just like Tom to see everything so glass half full. More like glass overflowing.

"Can you let me just wallow in this for a minute?" I asked, looking straight ahead, watching the snowflakes hit the windshield as we drove home.

Back to the bottle opener.

We arrived in Tortola and found our way to the marina, where we saw Pete. I waved and asked, "Permission to come aboard?"

He smiled and gave me a hearty, "Permission granted!"

I reached out my hand and he helped me up.

As soon as I stepped on the deck. It hit me. "I get it," I said under my breath. She was magnificent. She wasn't even moving and she was beautiful. Standing on that sailboat, I felt as though she were alive, like part of our crew, just resting while we stowed our provisions.

The boat was moored at the end of the long dock. She moved gently as the clear blue water swelled. I breathed salty air in the hot sunshine and listened to seagulls squawking. Looking up at the mast, I was surprised at how tall it was and felt dizzy for a moment. It reminded me that I'd only seen sailboats from a distance, really. Where they look like graceful sculptures.

On board though, she was more than a piece of art. She had a heart. And even tied up, you could sense tamed power. You could feel that all she needed was the invisible force of the wind. A day on the boat and I felt so much better about these new friends, no longer worried that my inexperience would diminish their fun. They made me feel part of the crew and not an outsider so different from the dark, cold, snowy night at the restaurant. This beautiful boat brought us all together. On board we were a team. A team that had just earned its first victory and had coolers filled with chilled bottles of Presidente beer waiting.

And so, it came down to this… an incredible boat with all the latest technology and features, a completely experienced sailing crew decked out in high-tech performance fabrics. Wearing things like specialized three-quarter fingerless sailing gloves, expensive polarized sunglasses, and Keen sailing shoes.

And me. Ironically the one person who would save our trip.

"Oh my gosh!" I said, startling even myself.

The group looked at me like *Huh?*

I quickly got up and ran down to our stateroom, where I dumped my backpack out onto our bed. And there it was. "Aha! I knew it!"

Proudly yelling from belowdecks, "Crew, you're about to get a big puff of wind in three, two…" and on "one," I appeared at the top of the stairs holding my old, cheap, mint green and white Reef flip-flop triumphantly over my head like a trophy. And there, on the bottom in the sole, was a bottle opener.

Call me 2 and 0.

Knife Flight

"Oh my gosh," I said, standing there in stocking feet. "I forgot. Isn't there anything I can do?"

The TSA agent held out a gallon-sized plastic bucket full of pocketknives and said, "I'm sorry."

I believed her. She looked at me sympathetically, with a kind of I-wish-there-were-something-I-could-do look on her face, but rules were rules, and my absentmindedness was to blame. I had to force my fingers to let go of it.

Even with all the hustle and bustle going on around me, I still recall the *clink* sound it made as it landed with all the other surrendered knives in a bucket of forgetfulness.

It had only been a couple of months since the new rules after 9/11 had gone into effect. There I was, mourning the loss of my little red Swiss Army knife, a gift from my dad, as we shuffled along keeping the line moving. Strangers all around me had their own agendas and could care less, just wanting to get through the inspection. Keep moving.

My purse, shoes, and sadness went into a plastic bin. There's no recourse. Either keep the knife and forfeit your flight or give it up. With tears in my eyes, I looked up at Tom for sympathy. He knows how I treasure mementoes like that, investing way too much emotion in them. But having to leave behind something from my dad? Oh boy.

"The terrorists just won," I said and blinked tears into the dull gray container I pushed forward on the stainless steel rollers into the x-ray machine.

Sitting uncomfortably in my middle seat, the excitement of this vacation had faded a bit. Mr. Aisle Seat arrived, plopping down next to me, cheerfully saying, "Hello!"

Turning and nodding at the same time, I shined a fake smile then resumed staring blankly at the headrest in front of me. Passengers continued to board, Tom was getting settled in next to me, and all I could think about were the memories represented by the dozens of confiscated knives in that bucket. Many were likely gifts or keepsakes of some sort. "I'm sorry, babe. It'll be okay. We'll get you a new knife."

"I know it won't replace that one, but I count on you to have a knife," Tom whispered into my ear, patting my knee lovingly.

Then he went back to looking out the window. He never carries a knife. Instead, when he needs something cut, he'll just say, "Let me have your 'knife-for-her.'" He called it that because it was dainty compared to more common Swiss Army knives. Only about two inches long it had one blade, a scissors, and a nail file that also doubled as a screwdriver.

The flight attendant was teaching us how to use a seat belt, and I was thinking about my dad. My fondness of and respect for knives came from him. He had been a knife collector with a large collection, including many custom Randall Made knives. They're beautiful like sculpture and are perfectly balanced in your hand.

Needless to say, growing up there was never a dull knife in our house. You could always count on extremely sharp knives. He taught me how to sharpen blades using a stone and oil. When he got a little older,

104

he modified part of our basement, creating a shop filled with machines to sharpen everything from chain saw blades to lawn mower blades. He contracted with a few local hardware stores, and when customers brought knives or blades in for sharpening, they were sent to my dad.

The MD-80 had been steadily climbing, and we were now reaching cruising altitude. I have to admit that my mood was lifting as well. I couldn't get my knife back, but I started to think about shopping for a replacement while mindlessly browsing the pages of *SkyMall*. I'd make it fun and enjoy the process, shopping for just the right replacement. Something to make new memories with, but one I'd be sure to leave at home when flying.

I don't wear a watch, I took it off the moment my dad passed away and haven't put one on since. Many people feel naked if they don't have their watch. For me, it's having my little knife in my pocket. Getting dressed in the morning, I put on my clothes, make a jewelry selection, and grab my pocketknife before flipping the light switch off. Ready to take on the world. Simple as that. Who knows what the day will bring? But if something needs to be cut, scissored, awled, tweezed, or tooth-picked, I'm ready.

"I'll have a 7-Up, please," I told the flight attendant when the beverage cart made its way to us, squeezing Mr. Aisle Seat a little too close for comfort. "Thank you," I said as she handed me the clear plastic cup along with a bag of peanuts. They were still handing out peanuts back then, before America and all her children were afflicted with allergies.

I wrestled the noisy foil wrapper thinking, *See, this is the perfect occasion for my little knife.* If I'd had my knife, I would have offered to open Mr. Aisle Seat's too, but instead his peanuts went flying everywhere when he got a little overzealous in his efforts.

The flight attendant smiled and handed him another bag. I tried not to chuckle, but I couldn't help it. We were both laughing when he said, "Well, at least I didn't spill my drink."

"Tricky to open, aren't they?" I said. He mentioned something about arthritis, and I was tempted to say something like, "Well, if we were allowed to keep our pocketknives we wouldn't have this issue, would we?" But I didn't. I kept it to myself.

He seemed like a nice man, but I weighed my flippant comment against potentially getting into a much longer conversation with him. We still had an hour and a half to go. The flight attendant unlocked the cart brake with her foot and moved down the aisle.

The wrapper incident made me think about how I'd used the blades countless times, opening everything from envelopes and packages sealed with that impenetrable packing tape, cutting up sausage and slicing cheese at our sunset beach picnics, and finally admitting defeat and cutting apart the damn bird's nest of fishing line I had created with a bad cast. The tiny little scissors had cut everything from a plastic hospital band they'd put on me when I went to the emergency room for a tetanus shot after cutting my foot open on a rusty boat seat, to cutting burrs out of my dog's furry paws after pheasant hunting — poor thing. In the woods I'd used it so many times I don't even know where to begin. I'd pulled ticks and splinters out of me and others with the tweezers.

Once, saving a drowning man, I remember feeling my right pocket to make sure I had it before we rowed out to get the guy. Not that I thought we'd need it for anything, but the whole idea is that it's just there waiting for you at the ready, like a golden retriever, only a lot less hair.

Tom gazed out of the window, occasionally glancing down at his atlas, tracking our progress.

I reached under the seat in front of me and pulled out my purse. I was after my pen to work on the *USA Today* crossword. Twisting off the cap, I thought about how the sharp nib on the fountain pen could be pretty dangerous, maybe even lethal in the right hands, like 007's. Would the FAA soon be taking our writing instruments from us? Pity.

"Hello, this is Captain So and So, we'll be landing shortly. Thank you for flying with us today and hope to see you on your next flight." His deep, confident voice made me think about the pilots killed on 9/11 and how that day started out like any other, pocketknives and liquids on board.

The flight attendants soon came by for the last time, collecting our trash. I handed over the ripped peanut bag. Giving up our pocketknives was a small price to pay, considering the many benefits.

We landed safely and uneventfully, eventually collecting our bags from the carousel. Standing with our luggage on the busy curb, waiting for Tom to pick me up in the rental car, I looked down and noticed the long white bar-coded luggage tags taped around the handles. Without thinking, I automatically reached into my pocket to cut all that off.

Dammit, I thought. No knife.

Jimmy Choos and Aunt Flo

My gynecologist wears Jimmy Choos. I discovered this during my recent annual wellness exam. Doesn't that sound pleasant, "wellness exam?" It's not.

"My hormones are all wonky," I told her.

"How so?" she asked without looking up.

"Well, my face is breaking out, and someone sent me a YouTube video of a cute kitten, but instead of deleting it automatically like I normally would, I watched it and tears welled up."

"Was it the one where it tries jumping into the cardboard box and instead lands on the dog sleeping next to it?" I hear from between my legs. She looked up at me, grinned, and said, "I love that one," then snapped the purple latex gloves off.

Feet in the stirrups, my eyes focused on the ceiling tiles, I said, "No, it's the one where the kitten curls up next to the sleeping dog, who moves his paw making it look like they're spooning."

Oh my God, I cannot believe I just said that. Even worse, I cannot believe I had gotten misty about it.

"Go ahead and sit up now," she said, rolling her little round stool over to the desk.

Scooting up from the awkward position, feet pushing against the stirrups, my pink tissue paper robe ripped, leaving me fully exposed. "Really?" I said under my breath. Holding a piece the size of a Kleenex over my larger-than-a-Kleenex-sized body, I asked, "When will this hormonal nonsense end?"

Looking up at me, still grinning about kittens, she said, "It won't for a while. You're not even menopausal yet. Hang in there. Get dressed, and I'll see you next year." And just like that, she was gone: Jimmy Choos, lab coat, kittens, and my modesty in a petri dish.

I balled up the pink tissue paper, tossed it into the wastebasket like I was shooting a free throw, and put on my clothes. I wasn't thinking about kittens anymore, but rather modesty.

I said goodbye to the receptionist and headed out to the parking lot. I beeped open my car and remembered a time when ladies my mother's age or older would whisper the word "hysterectomy." But nowadays it seems as if nothing is taboo, and people talk about their surgeries over lunch at the mall.

Bow hunting opener was finally here, and up north was all abuzz. Stopping in at the cabin of our good friend Tom, I'm greeted with a familiar, warm smile, a big hug, and a kiss on the lips. And while I know what he's going to ask me and that I could just give him the thumbs up or down, I let him say it. For tradition's sake.

"So, are you menstruating?" He looked at me intently. Not "How are you?" "Good to see you!" "Gee, you look terrific!" Nope, he's interested in where I am in my cycle.

"Sorry, Tom." I tried not to sound too disappointed for him.

"Well, maybe next time," he replied optimistically. Like what you'd say after realizing your lottery ticket isn't a winner. This issue of my period had become an important topic every year, no longer shocking me.

Inside the cabin, sitting in front of the warm fire *after* dinner, thank God, the entire hunting group, consisting of four men —and me — discussed his hypothesis: that I will be more successful hunting when I have my period. And does this give female hunters an advantage?

"An animal is an animal to another animal," I hear.

I tried unraveling that in my head, when Tom's brother, finishing up the dinner dishes, towel in hand, leaned around the kitchen corner and said, "It's not that simple."

Not that simple, I thought, *How do you know? You're a guy.* And for a fleeting second, I imagined Jack Hanna popping his head around the corner to explain why it wasn't so simple.

This discussion is always a serious attempt to discover the truth. But without any scientific validation, we always arrive at the same conclusion: no conclusion at all. With the dishes done, and the evening chores finished, everyone was back in the living room making themselves comfortable. The conversation continued more generally with a discussion about pheromones. Because of the number of shoulder mounts on the wall it felt as though there were many more of us in the room. Warm brown eyes seemed to watch us, and large ears to listen to our conversation. I wished we could just ask them and be done with it. Cozy in front of the fireplace and full from dinner, I gazed into the fire, entranced, hypnotized by the orange flames. I realized the conversation had died down and they were all just sort of looking at me, examining me.

"Stop it!" I said and picked up an old copy of *Field & Stream* from the coffee table. "Can we please change the subject?" But I was outnumbered: Testosterone 4, Estrogen 1.

Mind you, they were not goofing around in some childish school-boy way but were having a very real, adult debate about female hormones, pheromones, and wind direction. John added another log to the fire. I looked around and thought, *This is the same group of men I've listened to debate the designated hitter and instant replay rules.*

They were back on the subject, talking about possibly syncing menstrual cycles and moon cycles. I glanced up from the magazine and announced, "You realize I'm still here, right?"

My Tom never really participated in this discussion going on around him. He's mildly amused but that's about it. But this time, the conversation took a turn when Tom asked, "Well, if it can lure in bucks, what about mountain lions and other animals, like bears?"

Uh-oh, he just said the magic word — bears. This is when my normally laid-back, happy-go-lucky, let's-all-just-get-along husband jumped in to immediately quell this new take on the subject.

He leaned forward, readjusted himself on the couch, and said, "Enough of the bear talk already."

Here's why. I'm scared of bears, and he knows it. There, I said it. I've been in the woods alone and come across bears. Close. Close enough to see their eyes eyeing me. Specifically, I'm afraid of what they could do to me. Off the top of my head, here's a for instance:

It starts with a big sow cornering me up in my stand. Flight or fight has basically become checkmate, giving me adequate time to become fully terrified. She then rips me down to the ground, where I am bleeding from her claws and injured from the fall. As I'm lying there unable to move, the black beast growls a killer roar, as if to mock me — "You shouldn't have taken me for granted, bitch" — drool is coming out of each side of her muzzle, fangs exposed. *Why can't I pass out from fear?* I think as I try to scream but nothing comes out. Instead, I huddle, balled up, trying to pretend I'm dead as she violently begins ripping into my flesh. I lie there, bleeding profusely, staining Mother Nature's carpet. My last thought will be how angry I am because "they" always say to "curl up and play dead." So, not only will I die having been ripped to shreds, but I will be dying pissed off at the bad advice.

That's what I'm afraid of, and it's as realistic to me as anything. Why? Because I spend a lot of time in the woods. And someday I may come across a bear that I've caught off guard or I will have accidentally put myself in between momma and her cubs. So far, I've been able to manage my fear and tame my all too vivid imagination. Tom too, has done an admirable job, so far, of convincing me that bears have no desire to eat me. The boys continued talking, the fire snapped and crackled, and I stretched out on one of the sofas, thinking.

Thinking about bear fear. In cases like this I look for someone to blame, and in this instance, I am laying it all on my dad. My wonderful, fun-loving dad, who, when I was little, say five or six years old, would take me along with him to Burger Brothers, our local outdoors store. Inside was a huge stuffed black bear, standing up on its hinders, teeth exposed, one paw near its side and one reaching out with those long yellowish/grayish claws. Right as we walked by it my dad would yell, "Rahhh!" at the same time poking my ribs. Of course, I would let out a scream and jump. He'd get the reaction he hoped for, and I'd recover. He'd hug me, and then we'd shop for fishing tackle.

I'm sure I loved it because how could you not? I was with my dad, we were at his favorite man-store just knocking around, and he was giving me his loving attention. Gee, who could have predicted that repeatedly scaring me during my formative years in front of a huge, snarling black bear would have such a lasting effect? (Same goes for the monster living in the basement, the one under my bed, and the one in the closet.) Enough psychotherapy. I faded back into the conversation.

From my spot on the couch, still looking at my magazine, I could, in my peripheral vision, see my Tom giving the cutoff signal at his throat to Tom and the rest of the guys. Everyone has a bear story and with each retelling the stories manage to become bigger and scarier.

"Ix-nay on the air-bay alk-tay," he said adamantly, trying again to stop the bear talk.

"Uh, honey, sorry, but I'm the only other person in this room who speaks pig Latin," I said lovingly and nodded my appreciation at his effort.

He was worried they might plant some new fears about bears in my head, ones I hadn't thought of yet and ones he'd have to counter. If he failed he'd lose his outdoor play buddy. He didn't need to worry, though. Bears or not, I'm staying in the woods.

I looked up into the eyes of the buck on the wall in front of me and hoped I'd see one just like him the next morning. It's unscientific, but so far, in my experience, I don't think I see any more deer than anyone else. Although I do understand why my buddies are so curious. Hunters often use scent or doe estrus, to lure bucks to their stand locations. For instance, Cabela's sells something called Top Secret Hot Mama Doe Scent. The estrus is very effective for horny bucks, who can pick up this scent from a very long distance, like up to a half a mile.

You carefully spray or dip a cotton swab or something like it in the estrus and hang it from the limb of a nearby tree. The wind catches it and sends it like Cupid with a personal invitation for Mr. Buck. Only, *surprise!* I'm the one with the arrow. I want to emphasize the word "carefully."

Once you get a whiff of the powerful scent in your nostrils, it's there for a good long time. You can blow your nose, and it's still there. Instead of cotton balls, I use tampons. In fact, every time I unwrap one and dip it in the doe pee, I think, *why doesn't Tampax advertise to men during the hunting season?* Can you imagine? Intentionally going into a store, browsing the women's aisle for tampons? If they were smart, they'd do it. If Tampax were smart they would sell a pack of 12 in Mossy Oak or Real Tree camouflage-patterned boxes. Tampons are as effective and ready come pre-strung. Just sayin'.

Until Tom started asking me, I'd never thought of hunting during my period as a potential bonus. It's normally a pain in the butt. Well, you know what I mean. Cramps in the deer stand? Sitting in a tree stand 12 feet off the ground trying to be as still as you can, focusing on any little movement, any little sound, when all you can feel is the gremlin inside you trying to escape. Not pleasant. And then of course there's the bloating, the pressure making you feel like you have to pee all the time. Then, when you really do need to go, taking all those layers of warmth off in the cold woods is a drag. Advantage? Not so much.

While Aunt Flo still visits me, she's coming around less often. The number one benefit of not having her stopping by? Not attracting bears. In the meantime, it'll be another year till I see those Jimmy Choos and another year until I hear, "So are you menstruating?"

Easy to Moderate

"Why are we doing this?" I muttered under my breath as I tossed my gloves into the truck.

"Hey, I heard that," Tom said with a devilish look on his face. "We're going to have fun!" He winked at me and gave me the come-on-babe-just-give-this-a-try look.

Heading out to where we store our four-wheelers, I had no enthusiasm for this little trip. Sure, we had the help of a local ATV guidebook, which explained a little of what we could expect.

It rated the trails from easy to moderate to difficult. But nothing in that book prepared me for what happened. It was hot, and I'd vowed not to complain about the heat...ever.

It was a promise I'd made to myself when we decided to move to Arizona. I'd become a snow and ice complainer after living in Minnesota for 47 years, and I'd promised myself, and Tom, that I wouldn't be that person who moves to Arizona only to bitch about it being hot. Not me.

But...it was a little hot outside. I'm sure it was Tom's enthusiasm for trying our ATV's in a totally new location that overrode his appreciation for how hot it actually was that day. He'd even said, "We'll leave early in the morning, that way it'll be cooler." Honestly, all I thought about was if we left early, it would give the search teams more daylight hours. (Geez, did I really think that?)

For any potential search and rescue operation, I'm glad my ATV is bright orange. Not pumpkin orange or terra cotta. Nope, it's a color I like to call Come and Find Me Orange. The fact that I've given this any thought at all should be a clue into my psyche. I nicknamed her The Big O.

After moving, everything seemed so new. All of my surroundings? New. Everyone I met? New. Going off on this little adventure when we had only been in Arizona for a few weeks seemed fun and scary all mixed together. I knew we'd take our four-wheelers out sooner or later. I'd thought it would be later though, and maybe up near Flagstaff in woods that more resembled what I'm used to. I could practically smell the pines. But why I was less than enthusiastic about this fun outing was puzzling. I'd never thought twice about hopping on my ATV back in Wisconsin. Even on questionable lake ice. That never bugged me, so why now? I think the newness and so much change bothered me a little more than I understood. Why couldn't I be the super fun, reckless wife?

Woo-hoo! Let's go! Who cares if it's a hundred degrees out, and we've never been on this trail before, and no one knows we're out here! Why can't I be like that?

Instead, I packed my ultra-deluxe, never-send-a-boy-to-do-a man's-job pocket knife (in case I need to cut my arm off and later write a book that is optioned for a movie), my water bottle, a wad of toilet paper, sunscreen, a brimmed hat that I'd bedazzled with glittering beads, and, of course, my gloves.

In the air-conditioned pickup truck, driving the 60 miles to the trailhead, I thought about how I needed to show some excitement for this trip. So I asked, "Remind me again, what did the book say about this trail, babe?" This, as I continued to fold and refold my red bandana.

"Oh, it seems to be a good one. The book said it has great scenery and vistas. But mostly I chose it because it's considered easy to moderate, and I thought you'd like that."

Then added, "You know, starting with something tame for our first time." He looked over at me and smiled like he knew he'd done something good for us. I nodded back appreciatively.

"Easy to moderate," I said. "That should be nothing for an experienced rider like me."

Tom, still looking ahead, took his right hand off the steering wheel and patted my knee encouragingly, "You're right, babe, you've got nothing to worry about. Easy to moderate."

We arrived at the place the book suggested we park. The book failed to mention it was next to a cattle ranch, which meant there were at least ten million flies. Tom offloaded the ATV's from the aluminum trailer he'd bought in 1970, originally for his snowmobiles. I hid in the truck because the flies were so bad that I couldn't take a breath without sucking them in. Plus, I am, of course, too chicken to drive my ride off the trailer on those individual tire ramps. Tom checked the guide map one last time, and I told myself, "Easy to moderate." He gave me the thumbs up, and I responded the same. Everything was good. Soon we were off on the dusty trail. Wow, dusty. I realized I live in the desert, but holy cow. Thank God for my bandana.

Tom took off fast, probably to escape the flies. We were on our way, and since it's a smart idea to wear a brimmed hat (Thank goodness I have a head for a hat) I had mine on. But the combination of wind and the speed from my machine blew it off my head. Thanks to the chin strap, it acted like a drag parachute. You know, the kind that pops out of the race car to stop it. Only I'm not a dragster, and the leather strap was cutting into my throat.

Since my thick leather gloves were a tad too long for each of my fingers, grabbing the brim and getting it situated back on my head properly was impossible. I had to take my hands off the machine and throttle, which meant slowing way down and eventually stopping and readjusting everything: hat, sunglasses, bandana, and attitude. At least there were no flies. But stopping meant Tom was even farther ahead.

I revved up my machine and went as fast as I could. I needed to keep an eye on him as I hadn't really checked the map too closely. I was relying on him. But because there was no sense following too closely, considering how much dust was kicked up, I felt I was an appropriate distance behind.

We were still on a relatively flat, wide part of the trail, zipping by saguaros and cholla cactus. Then things started to change. Zooming

120

past a road sign alerting me to Mountain Curves Ahead, I thought, *It's okay. Easy to moderate. You can handle this.* We were already at an elevation higher than anything in Minnesota or Wisconsin. The open trail began to slowly curve. We kept climbing in elevation.

Soon there were points where I could no longer see Tom, only the dust from his machine left like cookie crumbs for me to follow.

The trail started twisting and turning more severely. I kept repeating, "Easy to moderate. Easy to moderate." I was doing pretty well, even starting to think how much fun this new type of four-wheeling was going to be. Beautiful mountain vistas completely surrounded by rock and cactus. But then on a switchback, the trail narrowed — severely.

"Shit," I said as I watched the trail getting skinnier. The chubby tires on my right side were beginning to get ever so close to the edge, and beyond the edge was a straight drop down.

I was trying to look ahead and at the same time look back at my right rear tire. Watching to make sure I had traction and a trail to ride on.

About that time, I remembered hearing how they sometimes can't get a mountain rescue crew down to you because it's too dangerous for the rescue teams. So instead, you remain at the bottom for all eternity. Your final resting place. I pictured handsome, hunky firemen, peering down at me from atop the mountain, shrugging their broad shoulders then disappearing.

I slowed way, way down. The Big O was purring and vibrating in sort of a rumbly way. Since I was barely moving and not creating any wind now, she was hot against my ankles where the engine is. Barely creeping up the incline on the narrow, rocky trail, fist-sized rocks would suddenly punch out from the knobby tires and tumble down the mountain. Tom was no longer in sight, any of his dust had settled. I now had to make a tight turn to the left around the corner. Off to the right of me was a beautiful broad sky vista like nothing I'd ever seen before, and directly in front of me the sharpest, steepest, narrowest turn I'd ever tried to take.

I hadn't realized it, but I was sweating profusely, and tears were falling down my dusty cheeks, wetting my bandana. I panicked and braked. In an instant, I stuck my right glove in my mouth, pulled it off with my teeth and turned the key, switching my machine off. Quiet. Since I don't ride with my hearing aids in, super quiet.

There I sat with the taste of disappointment and dirty, dusty leather in my mouth. Scared I was going to fall down the mountain switchback, I sat perfectly still. Sweating, ankles burning, weeping, and sort of holding my breath, I was figuring out how to get off The Big O. Carefully and awkwardly I climbed off her backwards, since there was no place to step off sideways. I kept my weight as much as I could on the left side. Mountain on my left, air on my right.

"Are you kidding me?" I threw my gloves as hard as I could against the side of the damn mountain like it was her fault.

"Why now?" I shouted at my machine. She didn't answer, which just made me angrier. I was so disappointed in myself. Was everything going to be like this here? Scary, challenging, and limiting? I had chosen new and hot over familiar and cold.

In all the excitement of our new journey, how had I not anticipated these feelings?

Tom got around the corner. Why couldn't I? I was hot now and so aggravated. Hot and alone and afraid that I had ruined our fun, adventurous day.

Know the sad part? Tom had done all the preparation, bought the book, got up extra early, fueled the machines, drove 60 miles, endured unrelenting flies, and I was stopped after only going about three miles. Three miles — that's it. The fun day was not.

There I stood like a baby, clutching the side of the mountain like she was my mother, thinking about my future up on that easy to moderate trail. Hoping it wasn't a metaphor for my new life. Is this what I could expect from now on? Was "easy to moderate" in reality "difficult"? Was my new life, my future in Arizona, going to follow suit? I told myself I can't be afraid of every new challenge.

"I gotta make it around life's corners from now on." But in the meantime, I dried my eyes so at least Tom wouldn't have to see that.

My penance? Waiting for the inevitable. Tom would show up, having figured out what had happened and, in his usual way, not let on that he might be frustrated or disappointed. Instead he'd hug me and tell me it was all okay. He'd tell me he was proud of me for getting as far as I did. I could hear him saying, "Next time, babe, you'll make it around that corner, I just know it."

Standing in the sizzling sun, my back against Mother Mountain, I slid down to pick up my gloves, and when I looked up, there was Tom.

"Don't worry, babe. You'll make it next time. I just know it."

Shark Week

"Are we lost?"

"We're not lost, Shannon. It's here somewhere," Tom said. He turned the same corner for the second time.

"I swear we're going in a circle," I said. But what do I know? I'm usually the one who's lost or at least turned around.

"Babe, we're not lost. I'm just looking for a parking spot."

"What'd we ever do before GPS?" The second those words came out of my mouth, I thought about a fishing trip we took to the Florida Keys in the early 90's. I've thought about this trip many times and not because of the fish we caught, but because we'll never know the answer to a mystery.

****

"Whoa," I yelled to Tom and gave my raised hand a quick flick. "You're good."

Tom backed the boat trailer down the surprisingly small ramp while I held the line. As he got deeper, our 16-foot Lund aluminum boat separated itself from the carpeted rails of the trailer and was floating in salt water for the first time in its freshwater life. I held on to the line and moved the boat over and out of the way, pulling it onto shore.

"Okay," I yelled and motioned with my hand for him to head back up the ramp.

Little tiny waves, no bigger than an inch, washed rhythmically onto the beach. They were quick, like a heartbeat. I looked down and instead of rocks and minnows, I saw through the transparent salt water, sand the color of sugar. I looked up and cast my gaze out across the Gulf of Mexico and thought, *Boy, it's a lot of water. A lot of water.*

It turns out we weren't the only Minnesotans down in the Keys escaping the freezing winter. Earlier in the day, as we pitched our tent and set up camp, we'd met two young couples also from the land of 10,000 lakes who'd spotted our license plate. They too had just arrived at camp and had brought a boat down.

"Have fun! We'll compare notes later, huh?" one of the girls said to us. They smiled, and I could sense we were all feeling the same satisfaction, smugness really, having escaped the subzero temps 1,500 miles north. Feeling refreshed by the warm gulf breeze after a day and a half in the pickup, I couldn't wait to get out on the water. The young couples

126

gave Rip one last pet, stood up, and headed off, giving us a "We'll see ya."

"You betchya! See ya later." We waved back to them.

"C'mere, Rip," I said and slapped my right thigh. "You stick around." He looked up at me but turned and watched his new friends wander up the road. "Hey," I said, getting his attention again.

This time I pointed at his new invisible boundaries that made up our campsite. "Got it?" I asked, but it wasn't as much a question as a take-notice message. He looked up at me like, *No problem* and hopped up into one of the lawn chairs to supervise.

"Help me with this for a sec," Tom said and pulled up the giant tent by two corners.

"Isn't it crazy that we travel all this way and the first people we meet are from the tundra too?" I said and grabbed the other two corners of our manila-folder colored, canvas Eureka tent.

"They're here to fish for sharks," Tom said from somewhere under the mountain of canvas. Then he reappeared with a handful of stakes.

"Sharks? What? What do they know about fishing for sharks? Why would you want to do that anyway?" I asked in amazement. Suddenly I had a very bad feeling in my gut. The kind of sick feeling that comes when you realize you're having a premonition.

The bad feelings weren't just in my stomach but in my head, too. I saw images of a headline: Minnesotans Missing. I felt dread. Powerful dread. We were a long way from home and a long way from fishing for walleyes.

I had only just met them, and already I could see them adrift in a boat, bloody chum floating and bobbing like disgusting garbage, and darkness falling on them. Our acquaintances stranded at sea.

"Not sure, I talked to one of them at the boat ramp earlier. Hey, help me here."

I stood there, frozen.

"Shannon. Hey! Earth to Shannon."

"Huh? Big boat? Do they have a big boat?" I asked still trying to comprehend this idea. I realized Tom was waiting for me, so I pulled the last corner of the tent cover and hooked it on the stake and jammed it into the ground. Then I stepped on it for good measure.

"No, not really. Maybe two feet bigger than ours," Tom said. He stepped back and smiled, pleased with our accomplishment. This would be our home for the next 12 days. "C'mon, let's get the rest of this set up so we can go play."

"Yeah, okay," I mumbled, still trying to picture two guys in a little aluminum boat like ours fishing for sharks. Bad feelings clung to me like the dog hair on the jeans I still had on.

We had our pickup truck, our boat, the bikes, rollerblades, and, of course, Rip. We'd brought fishing gear, thinking we'd fish all day and eat what we caught for dinner. This worked out a couple of times, but after discovering a little shack on the side of the road called Monte's Seafood, fishing for dinner became the backup plan.

We boiled water in our cast-iron skillet over the campfire and ate stone crab claws with melted butter until we couldn't take another bite. A pair of pliers from Tom's modified toolbox served as the shell cracker. Stone crab claws are tough, but it turns out we were tougher. Eating stone crab on a picnic table in the Keys, pliers in hand next to a campfire? It doesn't get much better than that. Gluttony is a sin, right? I promised I'd go to confession later, but in the meantime, gluttony served with drawn butter was far too delicious for a couple of campers from the prairie to practice in moderation.

We still fished though and ran into the other Minnesotans a couple more times, usually in the morning as we headed out to our boats. Their wives shopped in town or tanned on the beach. One time they stopped by after dinner and loved up Rip. They missed their dogs back home.

"How's fishing?" I asked.

"Nothing so far," they answered. Which made me glad in an odd way. I mean, I wanted them to be successful, but at the same time I was worried about them.

Tom, Rip, and I fished the water among the tangled web of mangrove trees around the islands. We used shrimp at the end of our lines. Who knew they were useful for something other than sautéing with garlic and butter? God only knows what kinds of creatures we pulled up. It helped when Tom bought a little plastic card at the bait shop that showed the different gulf species. When one started making a noise at me, I thought for sure it was possessed.

"It's called a grunt," he said and worked at taking if off my line.

"I've never had a fish talk to me," I managed to say as I looked away while Tom tossed it back into the water. Fish that talk? A little unsettling.

While we fished nearby, the shark fishermen went out miles into the gulf. Either I had become accustomed to the idea they were fishing for sharks or maybe I felt more comfortable fishing in the salt water, but as the days passed, my feeling of foreboding had simmered down to just mild concern. I guess I was having too much fun, distracted by everything we were doing, to continue worrying about the shark fishermen.

Stuffed with crab, we put out our fire and climbed into the tent for the night. I zipped the long screens shut and turned around to see Rip sitting on my sheets atop my foam sleeping pad.

"Go lie down on your bed," I said and brushed a sand dune off my sheets. When you sleep with a dog on the ground in a tent next to the beach, wiping away sand from your dog's paws is inevitable. It had become a nightly routine, like brushing my teeth. Once settled in, I leaned over to Tom and asked, "Do you think they'll catch any sharks?"

"They're pretty determined."

"I still can't believe they're fishing for sharks." With that I reached over and turned the Coleman lantern off.

"Goodnight, babe."

"G'night," I said and watched as the filament mantles glowed for a little while then finally faded.

The next morning, we got up early and went down to the dock to head out fishing. We wanted to be back before it got too hot in the afternoon. After all, we had to pack up. It was our last day, and we were leaving that evening. We saw the shark fishermen heading out too. Their time in paradise was almost up as well. Seagulls squawked and flew up from their roosts on the shore as Rip ran ahead of us to the dock to greet his friends. We loaded the boat.

"Good luck. Have fun today," I said to them and stepped on board.

"You too," one of them said. The other one knelt down and petted Rip with both hands and told him he was a "good dog. You're a good dog."

"C'mon, buddy, hop in. Let's go," I said. He jumped in, and I tossed the line free from the dock. Tom pulled away, and we were off, heading straight west, nothing but Mexico hundreds of miles ahead of us. Nothing to see but the horizon, where the clear blue sky greeted its bluer, wetter companion. All I could think of was *Boy, it's a lot of water, a lot of water*. I turned to smile at Tom and watched our wake getting bigger and bigger. I glanced at the dock and gave them one more look. As I did, the sick feeling returned. I twisted back and faced the morning again, wishing I hadn't turned around. There was no such thing as GPS in those days. No cell phones. Or at least none that regular people had. We relied on things like maps and charts, sound judgment, instinct, and perhaps luck.

It was our last evening in camp, and we were packed up and ready to head out. We had to get back home and had wrung every minute out of our vacation time, so we could not afford to linger much longer. We had just finished cleaning up our final supper of stone crab.

"Babe, will you put the lawn chairs in the boat? I'll tie them down." Tom had just locked the topper after putting the kitchenware and lantern into the bed of the truck.

"Sure," I said then noticed one of the girls headed our way.

Rip greeted her with his tail wagging him so hard he looked like a drunk who couldn't walk a straight line. But instead of reaching down for a pet, she looked at us and asked, "Have you seen the guys? They're not back yet and it's dark out."

Twenty years later, and I don't know the outcome. I want to believe everything turned out okay. But I also remember the presentiment I'd had, worried they'd get into trouble. We had to leave, we'd already cut our driving time too close. We never knew their last names and didn't know what town in Minnesota they were from. This all happened before computers, the internet, and cell phones. It remains a mystery, to us at least.

Tom drove, and as we crossed bridge after bridge, I held Rip in my lap, petted him and watched the reflections of lights flickering across the dark gulf, thinking, *It's a lot of water. A lot of water.*

Snowflake

One of the reasons I left Minnesota was to get away from the familiar. You know...there's a great big world out there and so much to explore. That and I didn't care if I saw another snowflake for a long time.

The day had been pretty unremarkable — a little grocery shopping in the morning followed by cleaning up the garage a bit after lunch. Rearranging some boxes, I was hoping to find some things I hadn't seen since we'd left Minnesota. The radio kept me company, and I was sweeping with the rhythm of a song when it hit me: my first dose of homesickness.

Well, let me rephrase that — cabin-sickness. It was a Thursday afternoon, and for about ten torturous minutes I was overwhelmed with the strangest sensation. It felt something like a punch to the gut. Like I couldn't see straight. I suddenly had this feeling in the pit of my stomach that we had done something completely irreversible. It was a trifecta of emotions — a mixture of confusion, sadness, and nostalgia all wrapped up in a nasty little package. It had been nearly one year since we'd moved, and I was convinced that since it hadn't happened yet, it wasn't going to.

But right there, in my dusty garage, holding on to a broom, it struck hard. So hard I began to weep. Yep, weep. I wasn't melancholy about my house in the suburbs, or even my family. I was feeling sad and blue about our place up north, what I considered to be my refuge. The sensation of missing the familiarity of the soft sandy trails, the lakes, the smell of oak trees, and seeing wildlife crawling and flying everywhere took over. The more I tried to stop the tsunami of emotion, the more powerful it became. Soon the tears were flowing down my cheeks. I was being consumed, unable to control the unfamiliar feelings, so I gave up and just let go. Part of me was embarrassed, and I set the broom back in the corner and went into the kitchen for a Kleenex. Bobby Jones joined me, wagging his tail and looking up at me expectantly, as if I might give him a treat. "Sorry, Bob," I said, sniffling.

I went into the bathroom to check my makeup and, sure enough, raccoon eyes looked back at me. Wiping away the mascara, still stunned from the unexpected hit I'd just taken, I wondered what the cause of this powerful blue feeling could be. Why now?

As usual, I blame my husband, Tom. You see, the previous Friday he'd suggested we take a leisurely drive up north.

"Hey, babe, why don't we go for a drive on Sunday?" he said during dinner.

"Sure, where do you want to go?" I asked and took a bite of grilled chicken.

"Well, I was thinking we'd head up north."

"Up north" in Arizona had new meaning for a Minnesota girl born and raised on the prairie. I come from, I believe, the fifth flattest state. As flat as melba toast. Here in Arizona, you're not only heading north, you are literally going to a higher elevation, so truly "up north."

Sunday arrived, and the whole family packed into the pickup. "Hop in, Bobby Jones," I said and patted the seat. He looked up at me, his tail wagging so hard his entire rear end swayed. He was happy to go along for the ride, just not happy about trying to jump up into the pickup truck. I reached down and lifted him into the back seat.

"You're getting chubby," I said.

"Who, me?" Tom answered.

"No, I was talking to Bobby Jones. He's getting a little hefty."

"Oh, I thought for a minute you were talking to me," Tom said as he hoisted the cooler in the back of the truck. We'd learned quickly here it's probably a good idea to take water with us wherever we go.

As we drove along the interstate north of Phoenix, I noticed exit signs for places like Big Bug Creek and a few miles down the road, Bloody Basin.

Sort of makes you wonder what kind of big bug that was, huh? Remember, I come from a place with towns named Cozy Corner and Embarrass.

Tom was driving, Bobby Jones was curled up asleep in the back seat, and the Diamondbacks were making an easy go of the Milwaukee Brewers. After seeing the crazy names of those places, I unfolded the giant Arizona map I'd picked up from my local AAA store just for this drive and began to study it for town names.

"Do you want me to drive?" I offered. "So you can look around?" I added.

"No, I'm fine."

"Alright. Let me know if you want to change up. I'm willing to drive."

"You just keep enjoying your map. I know how much you like that." I'm a fan of maps and charts.

The more I searched, the more Arizona came alive with places like Hellsgate, Skull Mesa, Skull Valley, Hellhole Bend, and Deadman Mesa.

Yikes! I thought. *Where did this powder puff move to?*

I looked up over the awkwardly large map in my lap and out to the vista before me, where giant cacti whizzed by. But my overactive imagination saw skulls and big bugs in a river of blood. I shook my head, hoping to get those images out of my mind, then asked Tom,

"What's the score?"

"The D'backs are ahead two nothing."

Miles and miles had gone by, and we'd made a pretty big climb and were now headed down a long, steep grade that curved around a mountain into Verde Valley.

"In a little bit we're going to head east to a place called Strawberry," Tom said, pointing to where he thought it was on the map.

"Really?" I asked rather alertly. He probably wondered why the quick response. But he'd understand if he'd known the list of places I had just read, only to be told we were going to Strawberry.

"Yeah, I thought maybe we'd get some lunch. See what we can find there."

With that, I once again turned to the increasingly crinkly map. This time I was on a mission. A mission to find places like Strawberry. Guess what, tough-guy Arizona? This state's filled with an assortment of cream-puff places. I found Punkin Center and Pumpkin Center. Really, two? And are there any stories about Wyatt Earp and the gang, after having too much in Booze Crossing sauntering into Coffee Pot? 'Cause there are both of those.

Like where I'm from, I found a Red Lake and also a Lake of the Woods. Although Arizona's version of Lake of the Woods is a little different than what I'm used to, which was water for as far as you can see.

Maybe that's where the heartache of my cabin-sickness came from, seeing Lake of the Woods on the map, a place I'd fished many times.

Well, the good news is those feelings soon faded away and haven't returned. You see, I found Paradise too — literally and figuratively. Nearing Strawberry, and before I gave up trying to fold the obstinate map, I spotted one more place-name. The one thing I thought I'd left behind: Snowflake.

Don't Get Me Wrong

"Don't get me wrong, I'd love to go," I said, feeling conflicted. "Love" may have been a little strong. "It's not that I don't like it, it just feels a little strange." Thinking to myself that "wrong" might be over-stating things also. Geez, why did I say anything at all? Then I told my friend, "It's complicated."

"Whatever. We'll meet you at one o'clock," my buddy told me, ig-noring all of the confusion in my words and hung up the phone.

I guess it's really a matter of convenience. Or at least that's what I think. I've done it before and actually enjoyed it, I guess. Sort of. Once I got over the weirdness of it. I mean it was so easy, comfortable, and convenient — hunting at a game farm.

We live in a convenience-based world now and have for a while. The first convenience I can remember was my mom and dad bringing home a giant box and putting it in the kitchen. It was the size of a small Volkswagen — our new microwave oven.

Convenience. In some cases it's great. Like when Walgreens came up with the drive-thru pharmacy. Genius! But was convenience a good thing for hunters? Was the game farm born out of convenience? Lazi-ness? Profit?

My experience at the game farm was like checking into a country club for a round of golf. Only more ostentatious if that's possible. The first time I went it felt a little peculiar. Well, maybe a lot peculiar. First off, I parked in a parking lot. A paved parking lot. Never before had I been hunting and parked in a lot. Usually I'm pulled over on the side of a road, a gravel road. A gravel road not identified on any maps.

I chose to not valet park my car. I figured I could walk the 100 yards to the door. Impressive columns of stone and wood held up a portico. Half slabs of timber were used as benches, and mini pine trees lined the drive aisle and sidewalk. A pair of bronze deer greeted me, though they were partially hidden between the baby pines and some white pampas grass. They appeared almost natural. Almost. A little brass plate on the wall as you enter the first set of giant doors with bronze pine cone handles displayed information about the metal artist who'd created the pair. Perhaps he had spent time in the woods or, more likely, he'd spent time looking at photos of deer in the woods.

The artwork seemed pleasant enough, and if you've never actually seen deer peeking through the pines, it probably makes you feel like an outdoorsman.

Entering the clubhouse, I was greeted by warmth, both literally and figuratively. The place smelled like leather and longleaf tobacco. Sweet, with a hint of musk and pine. I bit the end of my mitten, pulling it off my right hand, then I pulled my left one off too. I removed my knit cap while surveying my surroundings. My hair crackled and stood completely on end from the static electricity. Everywhere I looked, the walls were wrapped in a plaid of navy and evergreen with yellow and white accents. Wide oak molding wound its way around doors and windows and crept along the floors, guiding me down the hallway. Chandeliers made from what looked like elk antlers twisted together hung above me. Worn caramel-color leather chairs sat paired together, reminding me of old married couples. Brass lamps illuminated paintings of men in red coats on horseback with hounds littered at their feet, looking anxious for the hunt. I literally could feel the level of testosterone rising inside me, like I might sprout a penis.

Don't get me wrong, it was pretty. At the same time, I felt like I had walked into some kind of Twilight Zone. It was a tad overdone, but then I'm sure the interior designer was going for what he imagined was the feel of "hunting elegance." Do those two words even go together? Sort of like "sophisticated roadhouse."

Eventually I found my guys and gave everyone a big hug while trying to pat down my unruly hair. We checked in at a desk made from knotty pine. A pheasant, wings spread, was mounted on the wall behind the long desk, hinting at what was to come.

An engraved brass tag underneath advertised the taxidermist who had done the beautiful bird-in-flight work.

His business cards were available in a little holder cut from a birch log on the desk. Checking in, we were reminded of how many birds and dogs we'd paid for and the number of fields we'd hunt.

"Let's go," I said to the group, anxious and intimidated by my surroundings. I assumed we'd grab our stuff and head out. But when I turned around, everyone was moving in the opposite direction.

"So…should I get my gear, or…" I asked before becoming aware of the social gaffe I was making. But if anyone was comfortable being awkward it was me. This certainly wasn't the first time, and likely not the last. Probably not even my last of the day.

"Shannon, how about we get a cup of coffee first?" my buddy, the one who'd invited me suggested. He was pointing and motioning with his right hand, still at his hip, towards a room at the end of the hallway.

"Oh sure, that sounds great. Yeah, I could use a cup," I said, looking at his hand, trying to fit in, still stroking my head, trying to get my hair to lie down. I looked like a dandelion gone to seed.

I followed the guys, noticing how odd my worn hunting boots looked against the fancy wool rugs decorating the wood floor. As we entered what looked like a lounge, a tall man said, "Good afternoon, Mr. So and So."

To which I blurted out a snicker, thinking, *Mister? You don't know him like we do! Ha!* Once in our high back chairs, we enjoyed a leisurely cup of hot coffee next to a huge fireplace. The fireplace was so tall, I could have walked in it without even ducking.

There was apparently no hurry to get out to the fields, so I just rolled with it and joined in the conversation.

Our coffee was served in china, beige with small pictures of wild game on the cups and saucers. Mine had what looked like a ruffed grouse on it. Maybe it was a partridge. Either way, it felt elegant. I was uncomfortable. I don't own china like that. No one I knew had china like that. The coffee? Rich and hot, like my surroundings.

One quick pit stop in the ladies room before we headed out. The locker room had similar décor: oak lockers and brass light fixtures. Atop the marble counter was every kind of lotion and potion you could think of: hair spray, mouthwash, germ killer, hand lotion, Q-tips, mosquito repellent, and even Static Guard. Great, just when I'm heading back outside I find it. Pretty wicker baskets were filled with thick, rolled-up hand towels. At the end of the counter were smaller baskets with an assortment of feminine hygiene products. They even made those look pretty. This was all nice, but completely unnecessary. It felt like a salon. Don't get me wrong, it's just that we were there to kill birds.

Back outside we met our guide, who really did nothing more than drive ahead of us to the field we were going to be shooting first. We passed other fields with several cars parked. They'd probably started in the morning and were likely finishing soon. Our rental dogs jumped down out of the truck after he opened up the plastic kennels, settling down a few minutes after their release.

Pointing and drawing imaginary fields on the pristine tailgate of the company pickup, he explained where we'd be hunting first. We stood around him, watching then looking over to our field, getting our bearings. It was a great day in the field, don't get me wrong, just odd. The reason for the oddity?

Knowing there are birds hidden is strange, I don't care who you are. And knowing *how many* birds are hidden is even stranger. I kept count, but not of how many birds we had. I was doing subtraction. I knew what we'd paid for. So every time a bird went down, I subtracted it. Subtraction didn't typically figure in my bird hunting experiences. When you're out hunting on your own for real, or inconvenient, hunting, it's never about subtracting.

It's different, it's odd, and it's oh so luxuriously decadent. Still fun, even sort of relaxing in a weird way since you know the birds are there, the dogs are trained, and you won't have to clean anything.

I don't want to say it felt completely phony, but frankly it did. For those of you who have done it before I don't need to explain, but for those of you who have never experienced "convenience hunting," here goes.

All the arrangements can be made by phone or online earlier in the week. Similar to booking a tee time. Arriving and meeting your group, if that's the case, you are led to the fields by your club guide where, earlier in the day, the pre-purchased birds, born into captivity, were removed from their pens and driven out to the fields. Shaken, they are then stashed in a bush or thicket.

In our case, in addition to the pheasants and chukar we bought, we'd also paid for a turkey since it was close to Thanksgiving.

Now the dazed birds don't know it, but two, in our case, professionally trained hunting dogs were also rented to "hunt 'em up." Selected off a menu like appetizers, you decide what you're interested in having that day — pointers, retrievers, or flushers. It's your choice on the style of hunting you'd like to do.

Regardless, the dogs are familiar with the fields, having hunted them many times before. All we had to do was push the fields with them ahead of us. "Pushing" is just that. You and your hunting buddies all stand in a line at one end of the field far enough apart to cover each other's shotgun shot range. Then you walk at the same pace with the dogs ahead of you, shooting birds as they are discovered. Once you cross the very large field, you walk down a bit and cross the field again, making sure to cover new ground.

The dogs are going to find the dazed and confused birds, point or flush them, until you shoot them. If you've hired retrievers, those soft mouths will bring them right to your hand. If not, you'll have to bend over and pick them up yourselves. Stuffing them into the back of your vest, you keep walking, heavy with the burden of dead birds. In our case, we moved on to a couple of new fields. It takes a few hours. Like a round of golf.

That's how convenience hunting happens. Convenient? Yes. Sporting? That's up for debate.

Once you've finished your fields, the convenience part becomes even more convenient and more comfortable, to the point of ridiculous. Heading back in, you are met by your guide, who takes your birds. You let him know if you left any birds afield. He drives away with the dogs while you put your shotguns, vests, and warm clothing into your car and head on up to the clubhouse — where the fully stocked, well-appointed locker room awaits — to freshen up a bit.

Even shower if you like, complete with a dispenser of liquid soap, shampoo, and conditioner on the wall. Disposable razors and hair dryers are available too.

Sitting in the bar afterwards, enjoying a cocktail with your group, you recount the details of the day. Of course messing with the one guy who never seemed to hit anything (was his gun even loaded?) while waiting for your dinner table to open up.

Outside on the well-appointed patio is a huge gas fire pit and grill. The bar and dining room are beautiful, decorated in deep rich greens and wine colors. You sit in plush, oversized leather upholstery with brass accents. The massive fireplace, snapping and crackling away, flickers in the background. Since the owner of the place is into hunting all over the world, the lounge sports a crocodile. Yes, there is a stuffed croc in the room amongst the other mounts. Animals I don't even recognize, from countries I've never been to or likely ever will be, are staring at us while we enjoy our drinks and each other's company.

The room is large but feels cozy, although twenty or more pairs of eyes, trophies on the wall, appear to be watching us.

It's safe to assume that PETA will not be hosting its annual regional meeting here. In fact, I think a PETA person might explode if they saw the animals looking out at them from the wall. *Poof!*

The waitstaff is exceptional. The service is so invisible, you don't even realize you are being attended to. Dinner is, of course, meat and potatoes. Whether the meat once flew, walked, or swam, it's all on the menu, an assortment of wild game. This is definitely the place to order pheasant or duck. Something magical happens in the kitchen, because once it's plated it becomes cuisine.

An executive chef has prepared these meals. And yes, it feels wildly pretentious (pardon the pun).

Five men at a table near ours appear to be dressed in Orvis' high-end Barbour of England clothing. They look like an advertisement you'd see in *Garden & Gun* magazine. I imagined them speaking with the snobbish tone of Thurston Howell, III, likely regarding the economy, or how troublesome it was to find a new Tesla mechanic, while drinking Macallan scotch like it was water. I wondered if this was the only hunting they did. Don't get me wrong, but if the only hunting you do has a fence around it to hold in shaken and dazed birds, I'm not so sure you have bragging rights. I don't care how expensive your gun is.

After dessert and coffee, our guide appeared again. This time, he had bags for each of us with the number of birds we'd shot inside, only frozen from another shooter's day in the field. Our birds will go to tomorrow's hunters.

See how this is just a little strange? Oh, it's delightfully comfortable, don't get me wrong. Being able to clean up with towels nicer than you own at home, a cold drink waiting for you, a dinner of wild game that you didn't have to clean yourself, prepared by a chef renowned for his wild game cuisine. No problem there. But it does feel a little strange walking out to your car with frozen birds. Shake and bake, baby, shake and bake!

Contrast this with hunting on your own property, on someone else's who you've received permission from, or on public land. Convenience hunting completely removes scouting, which is one of my favorite parts about hunting and possibly the best part about it. The incredibly inconvenient process, the discovery.

This takes gumption and time. Learning the lay of the land, all of it: the hills, the tree cover, the ponds or wetlands, the wind direction, the moon phase.

All of the knowledge you need to be successful in your efforts. In fact, the definition of convenient is little trouble or effort.

Bird hunting, whether for pheasant, grouse, ducks, or geese has the added appeal of working with your dog. Hunting with a dog that you've personally trained and live with every day is an awesome experience. You have an animal who's bred to perform certain tasks, then learns from you what you are thinking and how you want him to behave. I'll never forget the first time I took my dog Rip, hunting with me and he retrieved his first drake mallard. We were such a team. That feeling is irreplaceable. Irreplaceable, and by no means convenient.

Pheasant hunting, and the same feeling. He flushed and retrieved those birds, loving every minute of it. Wet or dry, all that dog wanted to do was bring a bird back to me. What a bond. What a dog. The hours of training we'd put in for those times, so worthwhile and so much effort.

There is no valet parking in the woods. Imagine you're drinking warm coffee you made yourself at a ridiculous hour of the morning out of a thermos lid, not a china cup, while driving to your spot. Parking in a ditch, you get your gear out of your truck and assemble yourself while it's still dark out. Dog at your side, not knowing what the day will bring. Hoping the birds are there.

Relying on your skills is an awesome feeling. Spending the day walking, gun on your shoulder, dog out in front of you, not knowing if the birds will be there, but walking anyway is peaceful.

You're connected. Connected to Mother Earth, your furry hunting buddy, and something bigger than you — the knowledge that others have walked this same hungry path ahead of you.

Your dad, his dad, your buddies' dads. Spending it in a duck blind, waiting for birds to fly over, then watching your dog swim out to retrieve has the same connection. Only wet and connected. It feels like a gift, really.

Afterwards, walking into the nearby bar, complete with a bell on the door, an off-kilter pool table, and a jukebox for drinks with your buddies. It's cold outside and yet you're sweaty and steaming from working — well, playing — hard. Your friends have gone to the same amount of trouble.

And because of that, whether you realize it or not, there's a certain amount of respect for each other. Buddies who are not even aware of

Barbour of England. Who likely bought their camouflage on sale at Cabela's or Sportsman's Warehouse and got their dogs from a friend who had a litter. Leaned up against the bar, wader suspenders off our shoulders, hanging down to our knees, we shake dice and talk smart. Wet, stinky, worn-out dogs at our feet. No executive chef in sight. More likely beer than scotch and no frozen birds.

Finally at home, you clean up your dog, your birds, your gun, and your truck. These are what great memories, self-reliant, inconvenient memories are all about.

Now don't get me wrong, convenience hunting is a way to get out on a day when you might not have been able to get up north to your favorite hunting spot for a while. It's an opportunity to try out that new gun.

Or maybe you're trying to decide if instead of a retriever, your next dog might just be a pointer. Maybe you have clients who don't golf. Or just maybe because of age or illness, the alternative has become too much work. A million reasons to use it.

I get it. Trust me, I get it.

I'm grateful for the experience. There's a place for all of it, I guess. Shake and bake, baby.

Girl Group

Alone in my tree stand I was invisible. Silent and still, I peered down through the branches to the ground below, where there must have been six or seven of them. I watched for their brothers, fathers, or uncles, but none of them had wandered to my site. Just the girls so far, no antlers among them, foraging on acorns. They ate together and stayed together. When they moved on, they moved on together.

As I watched them leave, meandering off deeper into the woods, I found myself oddly jealous. A peculiar emotion I hadn't felt in a long time. Many years before, standing alone in front of my high school locker I twisted the black lock dial — 28 to the right, 10 left, and 20 back to the right. *Click* went the lock.

I pushed up with my index finger and opened it. I put the books inside from my last class and pulled out the worn textbook for my next. Like any school hallway between periods it was noisy and busy. And like every day before and after, I looked up and saw them. I peered back inside my locker and pretended to be interested in something as they approached. There must have been six or seven of them, the popular girls.

They stood nearby, talking and laughing while one of them switched out her books in her locker. When they moved on, they moved on together. They were all pretty, all dressed alike, with similar hairstyles, even. And most importantly, they appeared happy. I was insecure and because of that, envious. I wanted so much to be one of them. But instead, my social buoyancy rocked in the wake as their popularity crashed upon either side of the locker-lined hallway. The bell rang, and the rest of us shut our lockers and continued to navigate the halls of high school awash in our virtual anonymity. I know. It seems so dramatic, but it was back then.

****

Back in my stand thinking about the herd of does, I felt melancholy about my high school days and just how much I wanted to fit in with the popular girls.

But the sadness had a twist of embarrassment, *Geez, girl, you're 30 years past that,* I thought. Then came feelings of relief and resignation. I've never been part of a girl group and probably never will be.

As I looked out onto the oak and pine forest around me, I thought, *Really, Shannon,* this *is what you're thinking about during this soft time just before dusk? Maybe the fact that you're sitting alone in camouflage in a tree is the tip-off.*

I can count the number of friends I have on both hands. Real friends. You know, the kind that if you needed to call them at midnight to come pick you up, they would without even considering the inconvenience. But of those friends, perhaps only on one hand, are my girlfriends. You know, the kind of girlfriend that if you threw up because you had too much to drink, she'd be there holding your hair back.

Did I wish I had more friends and was more popular versus being content with the reality of being relatively solitary? Some days. Especially since moving 1,800 miles from that high school where I'd spent most of my life.

From up in my stand I've also watched solitary bucks. They appear majestic. I once watched a nice six-pointer who was about 60 yards in front of me. The wind was in my favor, and it still took him 45 minutes to come in on me. Close enough to where I'd even consider drawing back. Once he was within range, my heart pounded.

I had just begun to feel the tension as I drew back on the string with my trigger, when, as if out of thin air, a bigger, eight-pointer bounded in and chased him away. It was over in a flash. It was awesome to watch this all happening in front of me.

I only wish I'd had a chance to get a shot off. It's only once a year when the bachelors get together. Then it's mostly a big show of dominance. I'm sure you've seen it, pictures of them head-to-head, antlers-to-antlers, sparring.

I admire the lone buck's trust in his intuition. It keeps him alive. Bucks are careful, cautious, mindful of smells, wind direction, and sounds. It makes them a far bigger challenge to hunt. Bagging one of the older, bigger ones, the ones we call "Grandpa," is definitely a testament to one's bow hunting skills. Outsmarting him is very rewarding.

On the other hand, does move in a herd with a herd mentality, guided by a dominant doe. They are not as particularly careful about where they go in their girl group. When a buck is with them, still usually hidden on the outskirts of the group, they'll watch him for signals. But when it's just the girls hanging out, they seem to be less concerned and are calm in the comfort of their numbers.

****

Recently, I sat in our golf community's library space, where nearby in the morning it feels like Starbucks. Only a Starbucks with Tuscan decorating, and instead of Millennials, it's filled with active Boomers.

Golfers come in to grab a quick cup before they head out for their morning round. Others grab a specialty coffee made by the barista and enjoy the daily papers at little bistro-style tables.

I usually sit at the same sturdy wood table, floor lamp by my side, and write by the stone fireplace, which is surrounded by overstuffed couches and comfy armchairs. The walls are lined with shelves from floor to ceiling and filled with books. Most mornings I am the only one in the library area, where the stillness is punctuated by the sound of the espresso machine steaming milk. A few of the bistro tables may be occupied by men reading *The New York Times*, occasionally glancing up at the news on the muted television.

Somedays, my solitude is broken by a retired librarian who volunteers shelving donated or returned books to our library. It's a beautiful space and very cozy.

On this particular morning, a group of six or seven ladies came in. All about the same age, all dressed alike in what seemed to be a combination of cruise wear and country club casual. Carrying similar folders, each managed a hot cup of coffee. They began filling in around the fireplace. Smiling at each other and nodding in agreement about something interesting, I'm sure, they sat down. I once again felt invisible. Not one of them had acknowledged me, and I was less than five feet away. As invisible as if I were wearing my camo. I'd watched the herd come my way and, being fairly new, I sat up a bit and immediately put a smile on my face. A smile that I thought exuded *Oh, glad you've come to join me.*

Smiling and searching for anything that seemed like eye contact, I soon realized it felt like I was fishing, and my smile was some kind of lure. Only I was casting for inclusion.

I slunk back down in my chair, peered into my laptop, and realized it had become the new version of my locker all those years ago. Yep, I experienced that instant pang of desire to belong. Is it just me? Or does everybody have such an innate desire to be included?

And how much might we tolerate (wearing cruise wear, for instance) just to feel like we fit in in some way?

It became clear to me who the dominant "doe" was in this herd. Glancing over the top of my Mac, I regarded the group's behavior and tried to figure out the rest of the social strata based on where they chose to sit.

Oh, the poor lady who had to stray from the group to get a chair from one of the little tables, needing to put all her stuff down first. She looked sad when she realized they'd started their meeting before she returned. I gave her the benefit of the doubt though, assuming she was new to the group.

After only a few moments of watching them, I reminded myself that I don't have any of the trappings I believe are a prerequisite to belonging to the herd. I chuckled when I noticed how different I felt and even looked from them. The words to the *Sesame Street* song "One of these things is not like the others, one of these things just doesn't belong..." popped into my head. Yep, it was me who looked like I didn't belong. Dress alike? Not hardly.

It was interesting to analyze this group of ladies, all watching each other. It appeared as though some of them were constantly checking the popularity barometer, making sure not to upset the order of things. Ugh. Seeing that, I immediately felt grateful for my relative anonymity. I want to belong, but not like that.

The closest representation of my ideal girl group were the four friends in the HBO series *Sex and the City*. Women who liked each other for who they were and that's it. They didn't try to change the others.

Each different, each individual, and yet a group when they wanted to be. That's what I'd like. That's what I'm really jealous of. But I'm reminded that those four friends are fictional characters, created and developed in the mind of one writer.

It's not that I'm desperate. Just searching I guess.

Frankly, I've had more deep and honest friend relationships with men than with women. In particular, I love how the men I've been good friends with are kind, candid, interesting, interested, and you always know where you stand with them. It's simple. Guys are so simple. If they're hungry, we'd go and eat. Bored? We'd go do something. Angry? We duked it out. And when we'd had enough of each other, we'd leave each other alone. Simple. I'm beginning to think *Sex and the City* was modeled after men.

With guys, the relationship is usually about doing something together, not just what you look like or what you're wearing.

With men friends you share an interest, a hobby, like golfing, hunting, or fishing. I can't remember a time where we just hung out. The closest thing to just hanging out would be getting a beer at the sports bar to watch a game on TV. Even then there's likely to be a game of darts or Golden Tee involved.

Also, my guy friends will tell me things that most of my girlfriends could never imagine saying. I recall once getting out of my golf cart, grabbing a few clubs, and heading to the driving range, when I heard, "You look fat. Are you gaining weight?" from one of the men in my foursome.

Another chimed in without even taking his eyes off the ball, "Yeah, you do look like you're puttin' on some pounds."

It didn't even dawn on me to be offended. It was said with the same matter-of-factness as he would have said, "Did you know you spilled something on your shirt?" It's how they would have said it to each other. They were just letting me know.

"Got it, thanks," I replied and pushed the tee into the grass. Not once in my life has a girlfriend acknowledged my weight or size. Oh,

I'm sure they've noticed when it's gone up, but announce it so matter-of-factly and in front of others? Never.

Conversely, those same men will also tell you when they think you're the greatest and mean it, especially when you've done something impressive. For example, during a different round of golf, this same foursome watched as I hit my 3-wood stiff to within eight feet of the pin.

All of them helped me read that putt for eagle and wanted it for me as much as I did. They encouraged me and reminded me how well I had been putting all day. They said things like "You've got this" and "It's yours." Standing over my ball, holding my putter, I'd felt their now silent hopefulness as if they too were guiding the stick. When I drained it, they went nuts. Literally nuts.

Jumping up and down, they yelled, "I knew you had it in you!" and "Never any doubt!" This last from the one who'd told me I'd put on a few. The three of them celebrated by hugging me, fist pumping, high-fiving, and generally going crazy.

Because after all, it was an eagle — my first. Their unadulterated expressions of happiness stay with me to this day. Plain and simple. They just mean what they say.

I like men as friends.

And yet to this day, when I see a group of girlfriends together or watch as a herd of does wander unknowingly beneath my stand, there's a part of me that wishes I had that group in my life. But I'm not sure I'm ready to trade in my camo for cruise wear. Not yet.

23andMe, JB, and Bigfoot

A half a teaspoon of spit, some postage, some patience, and next thing you know you'll be telling everyone your genome percentages of this and that. 23andMe. The name's catchy, isn't it? I'm not the one in our family who's done any of the ancestory.com stuff or really have much interest in where I come from. But I'll admit to having watched with interest Henry Louis Gates, Jr., on *Finding Your Roots* on PBS.

For instance, Chef Ming Tsai's genealogy was traced back to his thirty-sixth great-grandfather in the year 891 AD. Now that's impressive. Makes me wonder if he cooked like Chef Ming. Is that in his genes? I'd spit into a test tube if it could tell me things like that. Any interest in genetics for me has been confined to the ancestry of one very important and impressive deer — the Jordan Buck, named after James Jordan, a Wisconsin hunter from a hundred years ago.

****

"Babe, it was a long, long time ago," Tom whispered from the driver's seat of the 4Runner. The SUV was parked on what might generously be called a dirt path in the middle of the Burnett County Forest. He was waiting for me to get my gear out of the back.

In a hushed voice, I said, "I know that, but wouldn't it be cool? A girl can dream, can't she?"

With that, I closed the back door without a sound, kissed him through the open window, and headed off into the woods to my stand and possibly toward a place in history. It's unlikely anyone's more optimistic than me during hunting season. I don't even care what season we're talking about: pheasant, duck, walleye, whatever, but especially deer season. Just knowing the Jordan Buck, which held Boone & Crockett's title of world-record typical whitetail for seventy-nine years (still No. 2), was shot within a half mile or so from my two best stands makes me just a little excited. It should. In my mind, the Jordan Buck's descendant had to be roaming around here still. It was only in 1995 that Milo Hanson's Saskatchewan buck was ruled No. 1.

"Genetics, man, genetics," I whispered to no one then looked up to the hunting gods surely watching me and asked them to breathe a little favor in my direction.

The story of the Jordan Buck is as impressive as his size. Any sportsman knows this about a kill: The hunt only lasts for a while, but the story you get to tell, that lasts forever.

In the case of the Jordan Buck, the story is almost unbelievable. The tale begins in late-November Wisconsin, in 1914. With only one round left, twenty-two-year-old Jim Jordan dropped the 400-pound deer near a small river, only to have it slide in and drift 200 yards away, where it finally caught on a boulder. After he recovered it, Jordan took the buck to the taxidermist, and that's when the real, almost unbelievable, drama starts. The whole thing played out like a soap opera, as the buck disappeared and resurfaced in the hands of a number of folks over the next sixty-odd years. Eventually good fortune settled on Jim and his buck.

But sadly, at the age of 86, Jim Jordan died two months before Boone & Crockett acknowledged him as the rightful hunter.

****

I headed deeper and deeper into the woods and wondered if Jim's buck had walked on this very same path back in the early part of last century. I thought about genes and hoped maybe, just maybe, some of his descendants were nearby. That perfect buck grew up right there, right in those woods.

I padded my way past familiar trees and through the dense cover to the base of my stand. It's a pretty spot with a lot of activity. Rub lines and scrapes were all around. I took a big deep breath of cold air and let it out slowly. I watched the steam rise through my gaiter-covered mouth then up I went. A group of does came in on me and munched away on acorns blissfully ignorant of my presence. That was nice, but my thoughts were on JB, as I thought of him.

I had, quite seriously, prepared endlessly for what would be a once-in-a-lifetime moment. I'd rehearsed it over and over again in my mind, how perfectly it would go. After reading an article in the *Burnett County Sentinel* about a man in nearby Siren claiming to have spotted Bigfoot, I'd also gone over that plan in my mind too, but that's another story.

Back to JB…

I'd be sitting up high in my tree, and as usual, without warning, there he'd be. Like magic. Massive. Regal. Then I'd see that pair of huge, perfectly proportioned antlers. Squinting, I'd double check what I saw. Could it be true? *Focus and breathe*, I'd tell myself. Followed by, *don't freak out, you're not freaking out, don't freak out*. Motionless, I'd watch him come in on me close enough to get a good shot off. I'd let out my breath, and at the same time, with one gentle squeeze of my trigger, JB's thirty-sixth great-grandson would lie motionless on Mother's floor.

"Take that, Milo!" I'd say as I climbed down from my stand. On adrenalin-wobbly legs, I would announce, "I've recovered the title for America, for Wisconsin, and heck, for Jim Jordan!"

From that day forward, the Boone & Crockett typical whitetail world record holder would be known as "the Shannon Buck."

I'm pretty psyched about having the word "the" as part of the title. It seems extra special, and it should. But dusk had faded to darkness, and the day's hunt has produced nothing. No bucks and no, not even Bigfoot.

****

For Christmas many years ago, we bought a beautiful print of the Jordan Buck by Ron Van Gilder. JB stands next to a doe in hoof-deep snow. The artist had surely spent time around Danbury because the background is so completely realistic it almost looks like a photograph. It hung over our stone fireplace for years until we packed it up, using more bubble wrap than necessary, and moved it to Arizona with us. When we arrived, we put it up in our new living room, but it looked and felt out of place. I'm not sure if it was the snow in the picture or what. The fact that it was 105 degrees outside may have influenced us. Maybe just seeing a whitetail couple in a desert living room was just too incongruous. Within a few days, I took it down. It kind of felt like a betrayal.

Sad, but at the same time, we were so excited about our new life. I guess I chalked it up to change. Seasons change. We change.

****

In 2017 my aunt sent her two teaspoons to 23andMe. The results left me remarkably unimpressed. Although I did have to look up Yakut. A few of the labels said "broadly this and broadly that" in addition to having .2 percent unassigned. Unassigned, really? Her results inspired my oldest sister to submit her DNA for analysis this past year. I hadn't heard the results, so I asked if she had any.

She sent me her username and password so I could check out the report on the website. It was much more detailed than the one-page black-and-white summary we'd received from my aunt.

I spent about a half hour looking through the information until boredom overcame me. No surprises. Just a watered-down version of my aunt and my mom.

Then completely out of the blue, I received a large manila envelope with a packet of papers from the same aunt who'd spit into the tube a year earlier. This time, it wasn't scientific explanations of DNA but rather the story of my grandfather. A grandfather I never knew because he passed when I was just a year old. I opened it, still standing in front of my mailbox, and began to read. And just like JB, whose story was so much more interesting than his genes, I was stopped in my tracks.

Her gentle letter explaining that long ago, when she got her first computer, she'd set out to commit to paper everything she could re-member about her father, my mom's father...my grandfather. Done, so her children and grandchildren would know this man. That was followed by pages of facts and anecdotes of his life. I could tell she worked hard to capture his essence and as his story unfolded, I felt I knew him intimately. But how?

Tears welled up, and I realized science is only a teeny-tiny part of us. It's not the strands of DNA that really connect us. It's our stories.

Miss Muffet

She negotiated her way around her web. I watched, mesmerized at the speed and efficiency with which she labored. Delicately, she lifted one of her eight legs at a time, purposefully knitting together her willowy web. Working away, she had no bother that I was there. Or did she?

She put so much effort into her afternoon, while I just sat on my five-gallon bucket, no curds or whey involved, mind you, just amused and impressed by her work.

I was alert to my surroundings, waiting for a deer, whitetail or mule, to wander into my range. In the meantime, I was entertained by this spider working so diligently.

Normally the sight of a spider sends me into involuntary spider shriek mode, followed by the inevitable, involuntary spider dance. Well, not actually a dance, more of a hop or two depending on the size of the little devil. Usually this is because it has startled me in my own home. After the hop, there's always the now-what moment. In a split second a decision must be made: Do I kill it or let it be? Let me rephrase that, do I call for Tom to kill it? Or do I decide to let it be? If it's determined that squishy death is imminent, I run for a Kleenex tissue or a paper towel. Usually by then Tom, completely unfazed, has it between his thumb and index finger walking to the wastebasket. Me following behind, asking him with a scrunched up face, "Why did you touch it? I was getting you a tissue. Eew!"

But now, in the middle of this tranquil forest, killing it didn't even come to mind. And I don't think it was because Tom wasn't around. But rather, with no deer showing up, it was something to watch while sitting on my tuffet. Hunting in Arizona is a little different from what I'm used to. For me it's a little odd because where I grew up hunting, you would see a lot of wildlife activity while you were anticipating a deer.

In northwestern Wisconsin, I would regularly see and hear chickadees, blue jays, crows, and an assortment of owls.

Occasionally I'd watch gray and red squirrels, porcupines, fox, a bear or two (yikes, that's a whole other story), and, oh yeah, deer. One of my stands was 25 yards off a beaver dam. Watching the beaver couple working was highly entertaining. Here, nothing but a big, dark, hairy spider.

With each gentle gust of wind, I noticed what looked like glistening tinsel strung from limb to limb and tree to tree all around me. Beautiful strands of spider garland that shimmered in the sunlight. It was iridescent and glimmered red, blue, purple, gold, and silver as the branches swayed gently in the breeze.

Motionless and quiet I sat. She worked.

Scanning the forest for deer kept coming up empty, so I looked back to my spider. Uh-oh, where'd she go? Nestled between two gnarled oak branches, her completed web was shining like strands of silk lace in the fading sunlight. I searched for her, eyes darting from branch to branch. No movement. Oh, great. The oak tree was only about eight or nine feet in front of me. At first, I didn't think anything of it.

Dusk came, and the orange ball in the sky slid down past the mountain, and everything went into silhouette. The pretty sparkle of the spider garland faded. Darkness had turned it instead into an invisible trap, a killing machine.

Paranoid I was now in her lair and was her prey, she had become stealthy and, in my mind, evil. My image of a delicate ballet dancer weaving beautiful strands of glimmering silk was now replaced with the vision of a ninja, hiding in the luxury of darkness.

Did she know the rest of the nursery rhyme? Was she coming to "sit down beside" me?

The heebie-jeebies quickly set in.

A gentle puff of breeze blew, a stray hair not secured in my ponytail tickled my cheek, and suddenly I was no longer Miss Muffet. Instead, I was Jack be nimble, Jack be quick, Jack jump over the oak tree stick.

Damn Visor

Leaning my gun against the wooden rack, I turned my attention to the picnic table and listened in to the conversation.

"I told him, 'I don't care how attached to that hat you are, we're gonna shoot it,'" one of the men said in his usual matter-of-fact voice. Then he changed his voice a bit to mimic the apparently whiny shooter and said, "But it's my lucky hat."

"And that's exactly why we're gonna shoot it," he said and looked around at us to confirm that his logic made sense.

"What the hell are you talking about?" I asked. I swung my leg over the picnic table's attached bench and plopped myself down with the rest of them.

"Oh, a friend of ours shot a 25 at skeet on Saturday, and we shot his hat," he explained.

"Okay, I still don't get it. Why?"

"When someone shoots their first perfect score, he fills up the hat with a few clay birds, throws it, and the rest of the guys who shot with him, shoot it up."

"This is a thing?" I said still trying to understand.

"Oh yeah, it's a thing," he stated firmly, telling us he's done it "a few times with friends."

"Is it only with skeet? Because I've never heard of this before," I said, adding, "But I don't shoot skeet."

The rest of the guys at the table all were nodding, like this was as common as Wonder Bread and explained it's for any shooting sport, any time you shoot your first perfect round.

"I've been shooting trap and sporting clays for years, and I've never heard of this," I said, as I unscrewed the cap on my water bottle. And as if it were happening in slow motion, I envisioned myself throwing my hat out over the trap field, thinking how cool it would be having my team shoot it.

Then suddenly, just as I saw my hat practically explode in midair, riddled with shot pellets, I realized, *Oh my gosh, I wear a visor.* I reached for the brim and pulled it off over my ponytail.

I looked around at them, all in their ball caps, for help. But no. They looked at me like I was doomed.

"Too bad. We don't shoot visors," the guy across from me said, sounding as if I were cursed from ever making a perfect 25. Almost pitying me for making such a lousy headwear selection.

"Can't shoot a visor," another said. He looked at me through his yellow shooting glasses, shaking his head like, *What are you thinking, wearing a visor?*

I haven't shot a perfect score. Yet. Maybe now I have the reason, my damned visor.

"Hey, I have an extra hat for you, Shannon, in case you shoot 25 today," another said, not looking at me but meticulously cleaning his shooting glasses. Wiping them with a microfiber cloth then examining them at arm's length for smudges. "I won't miss it, it's been in my car forever."

There we sat, me and four men in varying color ball caps with different logos, ranging from *NRA* to *Cabela's* to *Arizona—It's a Dry Heat* to *Shooter's World*.

I looked closely now at my black visor and realized it had *Taylor-Made* embroidered on it. "Geez," I said and dropped it on the table. I was wearing a golf manufacturer's visor and not even a gun- or shooting-related visor. I should at least be wearing my gun brand — Benelli.

Noticing my angst, the man in the *NRA* cap said, "Hey, don't worry about it, Shannon. I'm sure you'll do fine, and remember, we can loan you a hat if you hit 25 today."

"Thanks," I said, trying to make it sound like I appreciated the sentiment. And I did, but in my mind, I was thinking, *Loan me a hat? Loan me a hat that would represent my single best shooting feat to date? A loaner? Oh God.*

Walking out to the fourth station, Nelli in hand, visor on, I felt completely conflicted. Of course I wanted to shoot a perfect score. But since I only had a visor, and a golf visor to boot, they'd have to shoot some random stand-in hat loaned to me. Is some guy's hat standing in for my own hat going to take the shine off this tradition? Hell yes, it is. Then I wondered if I even had a ball cap or any kind of lucky hat. *This is not what you should be thinking about right now: your hat selection. Focus,* I told myself. And then, *Okay, Shannon, you really have to let this go and just shoot. Don't worry about visors or hats right now.*

Only, that's all I could think about. I felt like a misfit in my visor. I could feel it burning around my head. It felt weighty, where before I'd never noticed it. A burden I had strapped around my head. Like a crown of thorns. I had never, ever given it one minute's thought, but now, looking around, I noticed I was the only one in the entire shooting complex wearing a visor. *Get it together, girl.*

To my shooting buddies any arbitrary hat would work. It's just a hat after all. They'd be happy for me while shooting it. The idea that it would be a completely random unknown hat, with no personal chi, no connection to me at all, really bugged me. And God only knows what kind of karma was linked to it. How many people had worn it? It was his hat. Not that I'm superstitious or anything.

Standing at the fourth spot, where I normally start, I looked out onto the open trap field, mountain off in the distance, waiting. I was distracted. *Oh, for Pete's sake, Shannon — enough.*

Waiting, watching the first three birds fly out of the house ahead of me, and the men in hats blew them to dust. I thought it came down to the fact that I'd rather shoot a perfect score and have some random hat, than not shoot perfectly and wait to develop some kind of relationship with a hat I didn't even own yet. A random, stand-in hat would have to do, I guess. I gave in to the idea. You only get one chance at this. It's kind of like losing your virginity. You imagine how it will be, and then it's not. But that's the story you're stuck with.

There was way too much nonsense going on in my head, still wrapped in a damn visor. I lifted Nelli up anyway. "Pull," I said with her against my cheek. The orange bird left the house flying to the left, but not a hard screamer left. I pulled the trigger and missed. I never miss the first bird. Ever. My eyes followed the bird, and I watched it fall in one piece to the ground. I caught Mr. *Shooter's World* on my left, looking at me, I'm sure thinking, *What the heck?* My chances of a perfect round were over on the first shot. "Damn it," I said to myself.

I wanted to be part of this new (to me) tradition of shooting the hat. To be one of the guys whose hat's been shot. To be in the club. But instead of focusing and hitting the clay birds, I missed. In fact, I probably shot the worst round of the year. I'm sure the guys shooting with me were thinking, *Well, we're not going to have to shoot her stand-in hat today. Not with the crappy way she's shooting.*

I wanted so badly to have everyone shoot my loaner hat, that I completely fell apart, missing five birds on that round. Yeah, five.

Talk about busting my good average. Normally I might miss one or two, three maybe. But five? What the hell? What is it that goes on in your mind when you miss like that? When I needed — well, wanted — to be perfect. It didn't feel like lack of focus, it felt like focus overload. Self-sabotage? Not sure, but to this day I've not been perfect (yet).

That wanting-it-so-bad feeling. I've felt it before. Not on the trap range, but on the golf course. I've been fortunate to be part of many fun golf tournaments, where there's usually a long drive contest for men and women. And since I can knock it out there pretty good, I've always thought I could win the prize for women's long drive. The thing is, your ball needs to stay in the fairway to be considered for the contest. Of the 20 or so times I've competed in the long drive contest, I've only won once. One time. I can hardly believe it. But their drives stayed in the fairway and mine did not, even though it was further.

I get so wrapped up in the competition that by the time I step up to take my swing, God only knows what's going through my mind. Just like when I shouldn't have been thinking about my visor, all I could think about during those drives was wanting to crush it. I should not have been thinking at all. Normally, when I push my tee into the ground,

I tell myself, "Relax and swing through the back of the ball." Every time, that's what I say. My first and only golf instructor, Spanky, taught me to do this to avoid a mind full of swing thoughts.

It keeps me clear and consistent. I can hear his voice saying, "Relax and swing through the back of the ball."

But at these tournaments, my ego overrides my brain and I swing my TaylorMade Burner for the bleachers. When we watch the ball land in the rough or worse, the woods or a bunker, I feel like I let Spanky and my foursome down. Because they know I can outdrive most, if not all of the women in the tournament. I hear things like, "Shannon, you're in the fairway on every other drive, what happened?" The best way I can describe it is wanting something so bad, you "over want," and things go awry. In two words: I choked.

Every other time shooting trap, I never gave it a thought. But now, after learning about a cool tradition, my visor was the only thing I could think about.

Back at the trap field, I walked over to the rack and placed my Italian sweetheart down gently. It wasn't her fault. She hadn't let me down. But I needed something to blame. So I took off my visor and threw it on the picnic table, glaring at it like it was jinxed. I pulled my earplugs out, stuffed them into my shooting vest breast pocket, and replaced them with my hearing aids. Only no one was talking. That was strange. All the guys were putting their gear away, taking their guns apart, and putting them into their cases. Usually it's pretty chatty. This is a talkative bunch, and so I waited for a comment but got none. Not one of my guys said anything to me. They knew I'd shot poorly. They probably knew why too. The picnic table, like the United Nations, is made up of men from all over. These men are a lot older than I am. They've been around. So of course they probably do things differently. Looking at my damn visor made me wonder what other traditions, rituals, and customs I don't know about. What do they do with a turkey's beard, or its spurs? And when they shoot a buck, do they hang its junk in a nearby tree? That's tradition. As vulgar as it sounds, that's what happens. After they shoot their ducks or geese, do they keep the bands and wear them like charms around their neck on their call lanyards? I did. Everyone I knew did. Now I wonder why. Is that a universal thing?

We sat at the picnic table and watched another group of shooters. Mr. *Arizona — It's a Dry Heat* looked at me, and in his usual kind way said, "Hey, Shannon, are you going deer hunting again later this fall?" Totally changing the subject. I knew what he was doing, and I suspect the rest of the group did too. I took a swig from my water bottle and answered him. Pretty soon the whole table was talking deer hunting and not talking about hats or visors,

It's a 40-minute or so drive home from the trap range, and I'm sure I saw the road while I drove, but my mind was far away, thinking about all the different rituals we had and how I didn't really know why we did them, except that it was always done that way.

For instance, before heading out for rifle-season deer hunting, a pull of blackberry brandy was traditional. It was commonly referred to as "mother's milk." Inevitably, someone would produce a flask of milk, and everyone would take a swig. Then, at least for me, after a hard swallow and making the scrunchy face — eyes watering, lips pursed — we were off for the afternoon hunt.

Whether you liked it or not, it was a rite of passage: old or young, male or female, it bonded us and so you did it.

Fishing is no different. The week before opener my dad would always have me sit with him in the kitchen. He'd say, "Go get a pencil, babe." Then he would jab it through the new fishing line spool's label and tell me to hold it and use my thumb to apply enough tension while he wound it onto his reel. There we sat, just the two of us, talking about why he was using that particular test line on that particular rod. We'd talk about the upcoming fishing season, discuss where he wanted to fish that year, and tell stories. I'd usually say something starting with "Remember when…" and we'd recall the circumstances, laugh or get excited all over again.

Talking and laughing, he'd rig up the remaining fishing poles. An ordinary thing to do, but it was special time with my dad. We did this every year that I lived at home. It was tradition.

Back at my old trap club, wearing a pair of ladies pink panties on your head after shooting the low score for Team Gang Bang was a tradition. Someone from their trap team who shot poorly that evening was going to be walking around the gun club well identified the rest of the evening.

"Sorry, man," I've said to that poor guy while sidled up to the bar, waiting for our beer.

Then, grabbing his pitchers, he'd say something like, "It's alright, I'll get 'em next week."

Even humiliation can be considered a tradition. I'm not sure I'd know where I was if on a Thursday night at our trap league I didn't eventually see a grown man walking around with pink underpants on his head as if it were nothing. All because it's tradition. It's familiar.

Traditions are what I love most about hunting and fishing seasons and even a round of golf with my usual foursome. It's knowing what's coming and what you can expect. Relying on the familiar. What really gets me going is combining that comfy feeling with the excitement of new experiences. Today I learned of a new tradition — shoot the hat. I love it, and I want to be part of it.

I'm living for that day when my guys will get a chance to shoot my hat.

And yes, I bought a hat. A hat I feel good about. It took a while to find just the right one, not that I'm superstitious or anything. The 25 hasn't happened yet, but now I'm confident it will. I'm working hard to make sure it happens.

Not just refining my shooting skills, but also my thinking skills. Learning to let go of wanting it so bad that it knocks me off my game. The mind game.

When I got home from trap that day, I pulled into my garage and parked, took off my sunglasses, and put them away in their soft pouch. I took Nelli's case and my shooting vest out of the back seat and put them away in their cabinet. Finally, I reached up, took off my damn visor and placed it on a hook above my golf clubs - where it belongs.

Supermoon

Oh my God! I almost burst out loud. I managed to muffle my scream by squeezing my lips together. Adrenaline exploded into my limbs, jolting me like I was sitting in an electric chair. This was my most prized deer stand, and while I hadn't seen any deer so far that night, it had been very productive for me in the past. No way was I going to pollute my stand with a scream, ruining it for the future. Even if something did just leap onto my face.

Its back feet catapulted off my glasses, flicking them off my nose and onto the forest floor below, taking my right hearing aid with them.

****

"Hey, guys, I think we can see it if we move over here," I said and pointed with my five-iron in the dusky glow of the early evening to the other side of the fairway.

"Oh wow, look at that," Tom added softly, as if not to kill the gentle vibe given off by the pretty quiet of dusk.

The four of us peered across the tops of the vanilla-colored houses that lined the golf course. The sky was an especially pretty hue of violet and a sort of peachy pink color. We finished our round but not before taking pictures of our foursome with the moon photobombing us.

It was not only big, but once complete darkness fell upon us, it was noticeably bright white, as if God had also decided that switching from regular bulbs for the new LED type made more sense.

We'd just sat down at the clubhouse's patio when a young waitress approached. Her body was in front of us, but her eyes looked past us. Her body language emitted *Why did you sit in my section?* but we heard "Hey, what can I getchya?"

Without missing a beat I asked, "Have you any Supermoon specials?" using my best snobby British accent, thinking I was so clever. From her, silence and a look of complete blankness. But at least she was now looking at me. She apparently wasn't as clued in to the astronomical anomaly taking place over her left shoulder.

This was one of those times when I felt compelled to educate, when I should have simply said, "I'll have whatever light beer you have on tap." But I pursued it, and so I asked her to turn around and take a look.

"Isn't it something?" I asked minus the accent. Like somehow I had any involvement in the production of this lunar event and that whatever was different about the moon was really obvious.

"Uh, yeah, I guess," she said and peered over her shoulder, but only to pacify me. Then she looked around at the other tables, I'm sure wondering how it was she got stuck with me.

Tom, as usual, reading the situation, smiled in a way that said *I totally understand you just want our drink order* and asked for "A pitcher of Bud Light and four glasses." It's not the first time he'd been in the awkward position of watching me give a science lesson to an unwitting student.

"Coming right up." And with that she left faster than a comet.

"You know, we're all stardust, right? We're made from the same stuff of stars. Isn't that neat to think about?" I called after her as I watched her leave. I'm sure I sounded entirely too romantic about the topic of the heavens. "Oh well."

Enjoying the evening, each other's company, and the pitcher of light beer, we continued to gaze out at the moon. The fountains were turned off now, and the moonlight glittered like white diamonds across the little pond. We talked about our round of golf, relived the good shots and the long putts made. But we kept coming back to the special topic of the evening, the Supermoon. News broadcasts and social media had hyped this for days ahead of its debut, November 14th.

Before saying goodbye and while finishing up our beers, I texted everyone the pictures we'd taken on the course.

Driving home, we did not need the golf cart's headlights. The moonlight actually created hard, well-defined shadows.

Before heading inside for the night, Tom and I sat on our patio to further admire it, feeling somewhat obligated. After all, as we'd heard on the news all week, we wouldn't see another moon like it until 2034.

"Maybe we should howl at it," I suggested, rubbing my dog's ears while he rested on my lap. He wasn't howling, and I suspect he wasn't aware of much, let alone the moon.

"I'm heading in. You two stay out here as long as you like, then," Tom said.

"We're going to stay for a while. Who knows if I'll be around in 2034," I said offhandedly. Then I did quick math in my head and realized that wasn't as far away as I'd thought.

Bobby Jones and I lingered under the especially bright moonlight. I was lazily petting his ears and counting the headlights of planes way off to the west in the distance. They were lined up for landing at Sky Harbor.

"Bobby Jones, where do you think they're coming from?" I asked, adding, "I bet it's a plane from San Diego, stopping here and eventually ending up in Atlanta," sounding confident. Bobby Jones, uninterested in our little game, offered no suggestions. He never does. Eventually the planes floated by us and out of view. I sat comfortably in my fake-wicker patio chair, trying to determine if I could really notice that things were 30% brighter than usual.

"Well, the white of the concrete driveway does look a little brighter, I suppose," informing him of my decision. Just as I was about to announce that I thought the white furniture also looked brighter, he sat up and opened his heavy-lidded eyes. My lap dog had suddenly become a hunter.

Mumph, he let out quietly, barely audible. His jowls puffed up as if a little bitty explosion had happened inside his muzzle. His body stiffened. His eyes, which had been almost closed due to the pleasure of ear scratching, were now focused on something that had crawled into the neighbors' landscaping.

Under the glaring light of the twice-in-a-lifetime Supermoon, holding back Bobby Jones from bunny hunting, I was reminded of the darkest night I could remember.

****

Alone, sitting in my deer stand, I waited for my ride home. I hadn't seen any deer and had long ago hung up my bow on the convenient branch near me. I had taken my trigger off and stashed it in my coat pocket, making sure to zip it up. Replacing my right-hand glove, I sat. Waiting. Waiting for Tom to come and get me.

We hunt in separate locations, miles apart. He drops me off and I walk, practically tip-toeing in to my stand. Then he heads off for his late afternoon hunt. Because dusk seems to be the most active time for bucks, he waits for it to fade into night before quitting for the day. I knew it would be a while before he came to pick me up.

He has to get down out of his stand and walk quietly back to his truck, which he's parked far from his location.

So now I was just passing the time. Enjoying the precious evening alone in nature.

A black-capped chickadee flew in and perched on a branch near me. Then it flitted to another and gave me a *Dee dee dee*, as if to tell me it was time to go. Like a bouncer announcing at two in the morning, "You don't have to go home, but you can't stay here."

I gotta wait for my ride, birdie, I answered back in my mind. All was quiet now. The gusty wind from earlier had calmed down.

Even the annoying whip-poor-will I usually hear off in the distance was mute.

Through the tangled tree branches and facing straight west, I enjoyed a front row seat for the sky show Mother Nature was putting on. Almost every evening I make sure to catch this, no matter where I am. "Let's see it, sister!" I say to her or "Bring it on."

Sometimes I'll even provoke her a bit with something like "Let's see what you got tonight," as if that challenge might make her pull out all the stops and really show her brilliance. I was grateful there were only high cirrus clouds so I'd be able to see her magnificence.

But looming off in the distance was a line of heavy clouds, waiting like a curtain to fall on her show. Tonight's performance featured a bright blue that morphed into orangey blue then to a pinkish, bluish gray, with violet hitting the ominous gray cloud bank. The swirls of high clouds combined with the colors looked like tie-dye from the 60's.

The show was changing by the minute. Sinking even farther, the sun had set and the tree branches were all in silhouette. The sky looked bruised, as bluish gray faded to bluish black and finally just pitch-black. The show was over.

Well done! I'd give you a standing ovation, but I have to sit still, I know you'll understand.

Unlike the Supermoon or even just a plain old run-of-the-mill full moon, this particular night was a new moon, meaning dark sky and no moonlight. None. It was so dark, I could not see my own gloved hand in front of me.

There I sat. In silence. In total blackness. The theme from Final Jeopardy was playing in my head, while waiting for what seemed like forever. Slowly, quietly readjusting myself on my five-gallon bucket, I was trying to keep my butt from falling asleep.

It was cold. Earlier I'd watched my breath leave me and vaporize. Bundled up from head to toe, I had my rabbit fur hat on, a neck gaiter pulled up past my nose, and about four different layers of clothing on underneath my heaviest camo. Still humming along with the game show song playing in my head, I sat waiting.

Looking up through my oak tree, I was looking for stars. Blinking, trying to get the rods or cones in my eyes to see anything.

Also trying to get my bearings. There was no longer a horizon line. I was trying to make out a few constellations, but the thin clouds of earlier had been replaced by the cloud blanket; Mother Nature apparently was tucking us in for the night. It was truly the darkest night sky I could remember seeing. Well, not seeing, I guess.

With no city lights, or even the glow of a far-off town to light up the night, I was in total blackness.

I wasn't scared or anything, I'd been in this scenario of waiting for Tom many times in the past. I was just anxious, eager to get down. Not seeing any bucks tonight combined with the freezing cold temperatures and the complete darkness was testing my patience a bit. But no matter, I knew Tom was on his way, and soon over a warm dinner we'd be telling stories of what we saw and how it went.

My particular red oak tree was among many about a half-mile off the nearest dirt road to the east and about 500 yards from a brook to the north. Tall, mature, fragrant pine trees are scattered amongst the oaks and white birch trees outline and edge the stream. There isn't much elevation change here. During the day you can see a long way off into the distance.

The entire afternoon I had been entertained by a porcupine who'd meandered into my area and seemed pretty interested in something to my left. He eventually made a big circle completely around my tree. He wandered out of my view for a while but managed to come back again before ambling out of sight as darkness fell. Mr. Porky was fun to watch.

With nothing besides a blizzard of chickadees breezing into my tree and out again, he was the only thing I saw. But now in the dark, the birds were no longer calling out to each other. There were no sounds. I sat wondering where Mr. Porky was. I decided he might be in the cavity of a down and dead tree, in for the night. Carefully spooning with Mrs. Porky.

Then, a sound. No, not Tom approaching, too soon for that, but definitely something moving on the crunchy, fallen oak leaves below me. I was sure it wasn't the porky, since I'd watched him waddle off until he was out of sight. Also, whatever was moving about was doing so in quick little bursts. I imagined a gray squirrel.

Then nothing. I was ready to go home. I sent Tom urgent telepathic messages of *Come and get me, come and get me!* Calm down he'll be here soon, I told myself. I decided to take out the little lighter I use to help Tom find me. He knows how to get to this stand, but walking the woods in the dark can be tricky with no real path to follow. So I carry a little Bic and light it up when I think he is approaching, like a beacon in the night.

A year earlier I'd switched from a little flashlight after reading about a deer hunter who was treed, so to speak, in his stand by a black bear at the bottom of his ladder. The man ripped his clothes into strips and set them on fire to keep the bear at bay. That sounded logical to me, so I decided I'd better carry a lighter too.

I took my glove off my right hand and was reaching into the breast pocket of my coat for it, when I heard the leaves moving again.

The sound was definitely coming from right below my stand. I was trying to flick my Bic, when I heard more of a scratching sound. The lighter would only spark, and just as I tried again something furry jumped onto my face and leapt off my glasses and nose to climb higher in the tree.

Any anxiety I had went instantly to blind panic. I swallowed a scream and realized my hat, eyeglasses, and right hearing aid were missing. My heart pounded. I was in shock and freaking out.

What the hell just happened? and *Oh my God, am I alright?* raced through my mind.

How I managed to stay atop my bucket on a two-foot-square plywood stand I'll never know. I didn't know what to do first. The lighter was in my fist. Patting my lap trying to find my glove, I realized it too was 12 feet below me on the leaves. The neck gaiter I was wearing to keep my nose and face warm was partly in my mouth. My eyes were wide open, my glasses were gone, and I saw only black. I felt my face and the top of my head, making sure everything was okay.

I was completely discombobulated and too in shock to be scared. I tried to reassemble myself, reassure myself that I was okay, the whole time trying to not make any "human" sounds.

Then I realized whatever had jumped on me might still be in the tree above me. So I shook the nearest branch, hoping to scare the little rascal. There was another oak to my right, and I hoped that it had scrambled away there. But nothing was moving, and it was silent now. The only thing audible was my heart pounding. I couldn't settle down.

My legs were so shaky that any thoughts of turning and heading down the tree were out of the question. I didn't want to fall and make things worse or step down onto my glasses or my hearing aid. So I sat, trying to calm down.

I was slick with sweat. My hair was wet; my entire body felt damp. I was no longer feeling stiff from sitting still in the cold. I'm just glad I didn't pee my pants. That would have been the icing on the cake.

Again, I shook the branch I was holding onto to see if the little creature was still around. Nothing. It was just still and black.

I'm not sure how much longer it was before I realized Tom was headed my way, seeing a flicker of flashlight here and there.

Relief! I managed to get a little flame from the lighter, and he found my tree. Never before had I been happier to see him show up. We never talk in our stand locations, but when he saw me he realized something was wrong. He stood at the bottom of my tree and shined his flashlight up on me. I'm sure what he saw was the face of recent panic.

He climbed up to me, and I whispered as softly as I could that my glasses and hearing aid were on the ground and to please look for them. He climbed back down and using his flashlight found everything. He was confused. I was shaky.

"Something jumped off my head," I whispered to him when I finally reached the ground. He gave me a hug, handed me my glasses and hearing aid and took my bow to carry. We walked out of the dark woods using his flashlight. I followed behind, feeling safe but thinking about what had just happened.

"Babe, you're alright. I don't see any scrapes or anything," Tom said while peering down his nose through his cheater glasses. He looked at my face under the truck's dome light.

"What if I get rabies?" I said, feeling all creepy about it.

"You're not going to get rabies, now stop it," he said a little more sternly, adding, "I think your gaiter probably saved the day, by the looks of it."

"I'm still freaked out, you know. It all happened so fast, and it was dark, and I was just trying to get the lighter to work then *bam!*...I was a squirrel launchpad." I was rambling, which I do when I'm freaked out.

"Let's go home, and you can take a shower and get warmed up," he said, still looking at me while turning the key in the ignition.

"Warm up?" I had forgotten how cold it was. "At least I'm okay," I said, looking for a little more reassurance from him.

"You're fine, babe. So a squirrel jumped on your face. It can happen to anybody." He laughed at me, and pretty soon I laughed too.

"Did you see the sunset? How was the rest of your night? Did you see anything else?" he joked.

"Well, there was this porcupine..."

On in Two

I watched my ball sail through the air between the tree lined fairway at Cedar Creek Golf Course in San Antonio.

"Yes!" I said to myself as I watched it land on the green, thrilled I was on in two on this par four.

"Nice shot, girlfriend!" I heard from my buddies as their cart whizzed by. Their drives were ahead of mine but had landed in the woods on both sides of the fairway.

"Thank you," I called back, still holding my finishing pose. Then in a moment of arrogance, I twirled my club like the pros do after they they've hit a good shot.

Back at my bag, I exchanged my five iron for my putter.

"Nice shot, babe!" Tom said from the driver's seat of our cart.

"Thanks. I'll take my putter and meet you at the green."

He gave me a quick kiss and went on his way in search of his ball. This was all very pleasing — for once having to wait on the guys.

I walked up the rest of the fairway, looking back to make sure my buddies' shots weren't going to hit me. But apparently, they were still searching for their balls. I climbed the gentle slope on the left side of the green. I picked a nice spot in the shade under a big tree out of the way, in case they too, hit it on.

I was feeling a bit smug. Rarely am I on in two.

C'mon fellas, let's go, I thought and wiped sweat from my forehead. I readjusted my ponytail and feigned impatience. The first hole had gone well, and this hole was even better, despite the heat and humidity. It was early September, and I couldn't really decide if I was in hell or Texas.

A hidden choir of cicadas serenaded us, so I figured I was still alive and in Texas. I'd never experienced heat and humidity like that before, and I've lived in Florida.

Soon a ball flew out of the woods about 75 yards from me. When I saw Tom appear I yelled, "The game's so much easier from the fairway," teasing each other like we do. However, as I gloated about my great shot, Mother Nature was about to teach me a lesson in humility.

Something caught my eye. I glanced down on the beautiful carpet of green and saw red, yellow, and black under my feet. I was standing on a coral snake.

"Oh God!" I screamed and leapt toward heaven.

Instantly, I tried recalling the rhyme and was frustrated that I couldn't come up with it. You know the one, the lifesaving jingle that tells you if you're standing on a deadly coral snake or the just as creepy, but nonlethal, look-alike scarlet king snake.

What the hell is that rhyme? Red, black, red, now you're dead? Or black and yellow kills a fellow?

So rather than just extremely wicked fright, I experienced instant disappointment in myself for not having paid enough attention during our short stint living in Florida, where they teach you things like the rhyme and how to identify a deadly snake.

Florida is where I saw more snakes in a few short months than in my entire life in Minnesota, including the one I completely avoided in my eighth-grade science class.

I must have looked like a cartoon character, you know, maybe Fred Flintstone in midair with legs pedaling like crazy but not going any-where. And just like Fred — and because gravity is a bitch — what goes up, must come down. I landed smack-dab back on the snake. Which I used as a launching pad again. This time I bounded forward then raced across the green at full speed. I ran toward nothing in particular, just away, screaming, "Snake! Snake!"

In the lush, quiet setting of a golf club, where decorum is highly regarded, screaming, "Oh God!" and "Snake!" has a way of capturing the attention of your foursome and possibly the group ahead of you. Two golf carts sped toward me, while I tried to find a way to keep my feet off the ground. I pointed vigorously across the green to the spot where I'd stood moments before my Olympic-level long jump.

"What is it?" Tom asked and peered across the green into the longer grass.

"It's a coral snake … a coral snake, I think."

I jumped into the cart and put my feet up on the dash near the windshield. I couldn't stop rubbing my ankles. I had a bad case of the heebie-jeebies. I looked at my group for sympathy for my near-death experience.

"We should go look at it," Dave said in a bit of a devilish tone. "I've never seen one."

"Go right ahead," I told them from the safety of the golf cart, as if it protected me from the ground. Part of me wanted them to see it so they'd know I wasn't exaggerating. You know, so we could all share in the awfulness.

"C'mon, let's go see what she's talking about." Tom spoke calmly, but he grabbed his driver.

Approaching the serpent, we looked like a conga line, walking single file, following Tom. Armed with his driver, my husband cautiously approached the snake. I was second, and behind me was our friend Dave. Next was the stranger, our new golf acquaintance, Jim, bringing up the rear. It must have looked like a scene from *The Three Stooges*, plus one.

"What's the rhyme, you guys?" I whispered as we crept closer to the snake. "You know, the rhyme you're supposed to remember, so you know if it's poisonous?"

"How should I know, I'm from Minnesota?" I heard from behind me.

"Hey, Jim, you live here, you should know," I said softly to the last of our foursome.

"I just moved here."

"Well, a lot of damn good you are," I said quietly, but perturbed.

We tiptoed across the green and onto the first cut of rough and stopped. Just ahead of us peeking out from the longer grass, we could make out the snake.

Almost in unison came a collective, "Eew…"

Tom stuck out his driver — a Cobra, no kidding — and tried to taunt it. When he got no reaction, he tapped it, jerking the driver back as quickly as he could. We all took a step or two backwards, as if an invisible wave of creepiness pushed us back. Again, no response from the damned, evil serpent. The three of us hid — I mean, stood firmly — behind Tom, who inched closer. Nothing. He nudged the snake again, this time a little harder, which revealed two severed pieces. A perfectly clean cut separated the front of the snake from the back. The tension instantly evaporated. Relieved, we stood upright and stepped closer.

"Oh for heaven's sake, Shannon, it was already dead," Tom said as if I had overreacted after realizing I was standing on a venomous snake.

"Cut by a mower. False alarm," my buddy said, sounding disappointed, as if next time I should get it right. "What a pussy. A dead snake. Whatever." Then Dave returned to his golf cart to grab his pitch and putter. Jim followed behind, shaking his head.

I pointed at the snake and stepped a little closer for my own inspection. "I didn't know it was dead," I said emphatically, but my words fell on deaf ears. I just wanted a dose of sympathy, you know.

Something to take the sting out of the fright I'd had. An antidote. But they weren't having it. Nothing. Zilch. The guys were no longer interested in the snake.

"Hey." I tapped my putter to the ground. "I was actually standing *on* it. You can see where I squished it."

"Shannon, it was dead. It's not like it could hurt you when it's dead," Tom said firmly.

"Red, black, red, now you're dead, is that it?" I persisted and worked on the rhyme. "Yellow, black, yellow, dead fellow?" *Was that it? What the hell? It's no good if you can't remember the rhyme.*

I walked away but checked behind me just in case, then heard, "Get over it" from Dave. Good advice.

Tom pulled the flag out and set it down. They'd each chipped up onto the green and lined up their putts. My adrenaline had worn off, but I kept looking down at my feet. My ankles tingled a little bit from what could have been. I told myself to get over it.

Sometimes in life things aren't what they seem. Like standing on a dead snake. Sure it gave me a shock, but really, how lucky was I?

The guys laughed and joked about the different things they'd seen while playing golf, and I realized the value of having someone in my life, a friend, tell me to get over it. I laughed with them and felt my smugness return. A good sign.

They let me putt last, not because I needed the time, but because it was for birdie.

"It's all yours, babe," Tom told me with a wink and a smile.

"Don't let a little thing like standing on a poisonous snake get in your way," I heard Dave say as I stood up from my crouch. I didn't even have to look to know he'd winked and snickered at the other two.

I interrupted their chuckles with a confident, "No chance." Smiling, I approached my ball and told my group, "I've played on holes with alligators in Florida, bears in Wisconsin, iguanas on Key Biscayne, and once, a bobcat in Arizona." I took a deep breath in and let it out while I took a little practice swing, eyes on the cup.

Teasing aside now, my buddy said, "Don't let that snake take your bird."

I eased my putter back and followed through.

"Nice shot, girlfriend."

BEN AVERY CLAYBUSTERS

1

Trap Score Sheet

FIELD # *12*

Team# Holy Trap

Team   Holy Trap   Date   7/15/2015   Puller   _____   Team Captain

NAME	1	2	3	4	5	6	7	8	9	10	11	12	13	14	15	16	17	18	19	20	21	22	23	24	25	Total
																										25
																										22
																										19
																										23
																										24

Defeat Heat

I pulled into the gravel parking spot in front of trap field number 12 between four white pickup trucks who'd all backed in. Not sure exactly why they do that, but they do. I saw my team, Holy Trap, assembled at the shaded picnic table. Before I got out, I peeked at the dashboard thermometer — 115 degrees. *Am I a glutton for punishment?* I wondered.

I turned the key and pulled it from the ignition, stashing it in my left pocket (always the left pocket, not that I'm superstitious or anything). Then I grabbed my water, my boxes of shells, and my shotgun Nelli. Reaching for my little Italian honey, I said to her what I always do, *"Pronto?"* Ready?   (Again, not that I'm superstitious or anything.) Hands and arms full, I hip checked the door shut. It was 5:30 in the afternoon, July15th and we were about to shoot our last two rounds of the season.

"Hey," I said, acknowledging my teammates. It came out a little duller than intended, but it was so hot out. I set my stuff down on the picnic table.

"Hey," came back at me in unison from the men on my team, sounding just as sluggish. No one bothered to look up; they were all fiddling with their gear.

These guys are good. Really good. Paul, our captain, is Top Gun. But I'm good too. And I like it. I know, I know, some may see it as ego. Where did this love of self come from? Not sure, but I've always been skilled. I think of my confidence differently from arrogance because I'm not jamming it in anyone's face. I'm just good. It's like a fact. If I were arrogant, I'd be making sure those around me knew just how talented I am. But I'm so good, I didn't even think about checking the standings. I never did with my trap league in Minnesota, so why would I start checking it now in Arizona?

I took one last swig from my Dasani water bottle, which, earlier in the day, I'd put in the freezer. It was partially melted and had what looked like a mini ice-tornado inside. Then I hooked my golf towel to the left front belt loop of my shorts.

Besides the obvious equipment needed for shooting trap, on an exceptionally hot early evening like that night, my golf towel is essential. It's an old one that I bought years ago at the Cialis Western Open golf tournament just outside of Chicago. I got it for a song. There was an entire bin of golf towels, hats, and visors marked 50% to 75% off on the last day of the tournament. Gee, who could have predicted that promotional items sponsored by an erectile dysfunction drug wouldn't sell to the predominantly middle-aged men making up the gallery? I use it to wipe off the sweat, so I don't slip on Nelli's wood barrel.

Standing at the fifth station I waited for my turn to shoot. Quietly, I asked Nelli, *"Pronto? Ready?"* She prefers Italian but is working on her English. Shooting went quickly. We're an experienced team. I'd been perfect through eight, then missed the ninth clay bird. A hard-left screamer from the first station. *Hmm* is really all that went through my mind. I wiped my left hand on the ED towel. No sense in beating myself up. I shot low, under it. I couldn't do anything about that miss. But at least I knew why I missed. Plus, I had more to shoot. It had taken me a while of league shooting before I could get to that place. The place where I focus on hits, rather than any missed shots.

I gave Nelli a little squeeze and thought, *C'mon sweetheart, help me out.* Bello e facile. Nice and easy. It had come around to me again. And, again I vaporized it.

"Pull," I said and covered the last bird. It disintegrated. Orangish dust blew away with the hot breeze. I was happy. Hot, but happy. I finished the round without another miss.

I shot another 24 during the second round. Afterwards, back at the picnic table Paul reminded me that I'd missed a week during the season, so I could shoot another two rounds tonight. "Or if you want, I can use your average," he offered.

The instant he said that, I kinda froze. I looked at him but saw the future. I just felt like those words were going haunt me. But even though it felt like time was standing still, hammering home the importance of this decision, it wasn't, and Paul raised his eyebrows for an answer.

"Uh…" I tried responding to Paul, but that's all that came out.I leaned Nelli into my body, resting her on my hip, holding her upright. She was hot from firing. I used the towel again and wiped my forehead. My arms and legs were shiny from sweat, and dust began to cling to me. I remember thinking I was glad my shooting vest hung as low as it did, covering parts of me that no one needs to see sweaty. I felt as though I were melting when I finally replied, "Ya know, why don't you just use my average?" I can't believe I said that. But I was unable to stop myself.

The relentless breeze blew on us like a blast furnace out there in the wide-open area. Paul tried blinking a combination of sand and sweat from his eyes. He gestured toward the neighboring field, number three, looked back at me, and said, "Well, there's another shooter who needs to make up a couple of rounds too. If you want, you can shoot together."

Nelli began to fidget and was sliding down from dampness, so I quickly set her on the rack nearby. I took a deep breath and wiped both hands on my vest and shorts trying to dry them.

I swear I heard through a mixture of Italian and broken English, "I'm *pronto. Sì*, let's do this!" I looked over at the random guy on the other trap field, then back to Paul, and said the words I would later regret, "Nah, just use my average. I'm hot."

"Yeah, okay it's hot out. We'll see ya. Good shooting."

Average? Nothing about me is average. What was I thinking? I clearly wasn't. My id was screaming, "What the hell? Shoot! Average? How about awesome? You're awesome, don't take average. Spit that word out of your vocabulary, girlfriend. You're on fire tonight! You nailed 48 of 50 birds. Shoot. Don't settle."

But hot Shannon ignored awesome Shannon, and I placed a still protesting Nelli in her padded gun case. *"No, spariamo! Stai facendo un errore."* No, let's shoot, you're making a mistake.

I paid no attention to the muffled cries as I placed her on the seat and shut the back door.

I got into my oven, I mean my car, and headed home. The air-conditioning fan was set to wind tunnel speed, which tuned out any objections, in English or Italian, from the back seat. Another season finished.

****

A long, shiny ponytail cascaded from the back of her NRA ball cap. It swayed back and forth as she walked excitedly toward the podium at the front of the ballroom to accept the first place trophy at our banquet a few weeks later. She posed with the presenter and flashed a lovely, warm smile toward the photographer. This would be a pretty picture for the newsletter.

"Wha…what just happened?" I said out loud.

I sat frozen. Stunned, trying to make sense of what was happening. Was I in some sort of alternate universe? The room warped and contorted. My mind backtracked though ten weeks of shooting and scores. This had to be some sort of math mistake. My team sat with me but clapped for some new first place shooter, the new Top Gun. How could this have happened? Had I taken my awesomeness for granted and just assumed I'd stay in first place? How could I not have anticipated this result? Was it something deeper, some kind of emotional self-destruction? It had to have been more than just the heat. Or was it? A million things went through my mind.

Paul leaned over to me, sort of shrugged his shoulders, and said something, but all I heard was, "I used your average."

I felt a chill. There's that word — average. Next, I felt an elbow into my arm. Paul said, "Shannon, go up and get your second place trophy."

"Huh?"

I felt myself becoming an observer, outside of my body, floating overhead, as if I were watching all this taking place. This was the premonition I'd had that last night at trap. In that split second my mind had recognized that I'd known something was going to happen in the future. THIS was that future. Me taking second place.

I watched as the room of shooters applauded for me when I walked up to receive the second place trophy.

Why are you clapping? This is a mistake.

When I finally reached the podium, I heard myself say, "Thank you."

I was given a tiny little trophy that consisted of a teeny little bald eagle, its wings spread open. Below its claws, a plaque where, engraved, was the word "Average." I blinked and blinked again and finally read the word "2nd." There was a flash, but I must've still been looking down at my trinket for averageness because the photographer asked me to look up and mouthed the word "smile."

I'd let heat defeat me. Or had it been something else? On what felt like a walk of shame back to my seat, I realized I'd ignored my own feelings and Nelli's pleadings. I should have shot that night. I would have beaten my average.

I plopped down in my chair and said, "Hey" to my guys, then I put the tiny trophy down in front of my dinner plate.

"Hey," they said in unison but didn't bother to look up.

The banquet continued. I sat distracted, reworking my attitude. I spun the trophy around so I couldn't see the word "2nd" and told myself, *Shake it off, you're still awesome.*

After the awards were handed out and the speeches concluded, everyone got up to leave. Without Nelli by my side, I used my phone and Googled "English to Italian translation." Then, instead of taking off right away, I went over to Miss Top Gun and told her, "*Complementi, ben fatto!*" Congratulations, well done!

Wonder Bread

"Tom, look over there." I pointed to the right, not even trying to be discreet. We were meandering through a farmer's market in Scottsdale. We'd been at the Parada Del Sol parade but left our curbside seats after the golden retriever rescue unit with about fifty goldens marched — well, tail-wagged — past us. I figured nothing could top that, so we moved on to the farmer's market.

"What am I looking at?"

"Are you kidding? Check out the millennial couple and their spawn."

The trim young couple wore slim-fitting, moisture-wicking black athletic wear. I think it's called "athleisure." Each had on a black ball cap; hers had a smooth blond ponytail exiting the back. Both wore what looked like expensive sunglasses, Maui Jim's or something. She removed her long-sleeved zip-up, folded it neatly, then tucked it into a compartment of the baby's sleek three-wheeled stroller. *She probably jogs behind it while an app counts her steps.* She slathered on sunscreen the moment she took off her fleece top, careful not to get any on her iWatch. Dad was busy talking on his iPhone, but then he used it to pay for the organic, locally sourced, non-GMO (according to the booth's sign) bread.

Mom knelt down in front of the black stroller and began taking pictures of the child after wiping the remains of her lotion on the kid's cheeks. Coaxing a smile, she got the shot she wanted. It wiggled and kicked its Keen-sandaled feet, but the kid smiled on command. This wasn't its first rodeo. Because the kid, also dressed in black, wore dark toddler-sized sunglasses and a black ball cap, I couldn't tell what brand it was — girl or boy. Nor could I see its wrists but imagined there was an iWatch there as well.

"I've seen enough," I said and smiled at Tom, who wasn't looking at them. He was more interested in the vendor selling 42 kinds of salsas at the next table.

"What? Should we get some salsa?" he asked.

I sighed, Salsa was the last thing on my mind. Why had I been so judgy? That was easy: They looked too perfect. All that technology, sheesh. It made me wonder what's next?

****

"Shanny, hold still."

I was five years old and fidgety. My mom crouched down in front of me trying to get me to step into Wonder Bread bags before putting my wool-socked feet into my knee-high moon boots. She'd already helped me into my snow pants, which were really just insulated bib overalls.

"Point your toes," she told me while stuffing my bagged feet into the puffy boots along with the pant legs. I wiggled and pushed, hands on her shoulders to steady myself as I tried with her to get all that smooshed down deep inside the boots. I just wanted to get outside and play in the snowy wonderland that was our backyard.

"Hold still," she told me one more time.

Eventually, my feet were in, my ski cap was on, and she'd wound a scarf over my mouth and nose, tying it off in the back. My mittens were attached to each other by a long crocheted string threaded through my sleeves and hanging out the cuffs. They dangled like forgetfulness charms, but at least I wouldn't lose them. The coat was a giant nylon, fiber-filled puff-ball so stuffed my arms could never hang straight down.

At last I was dressed. Mom stood up, let out a deep sigh, and with her hands still on my shoulders, turned me around.

She opened the kitchen door then pushed the screen door, which flew open and smacked the side of the house. Out I went.

"Have fun," she said, and the doors shut behind me.

No more than twenty minutes later, I came back inside and yelled through my scarf, "Mommy, I have to go potty."

"Oh, Shanny…"

****

The day after the parade, the always highly anticipated L.L. Bean catalog (hear the harp music?) arrived. I turned my phone off, grabbed a cocktail, and began to wander through the pages. I dived in like it was a storybook taking me on a much-loved adventure with really well-dressed outdoorsy people.

The tale took an unexpected turn when there, on the familiar pages, were clothes designed to keep bugs away. *Huh? That's a thing? When did that become a thing?* Clothing laced with something called "permethrin." Really? Do I want to buy clothing that has permethrin in it?

My mind raced with a million questions. What happens when you wash it? How many times can you wash it before it becomes just another shirt? What happens to the permethrin? Where does it go? What happens when you sweat? Does the chemical end up soaking into your skin? How long a life does it have? Does the permethrin end up in your washer? What kind of side effects does it have? Oh sure, the bugs are kept at bay, but you've grown another arm out the middle of your back. Isn't that what bug juice is for?

I read on.

The Bean ad said, "With the help of Burlington Labs, these garments are evenly treated with permethrin, a synthetic form of a naturally occurring bug repellent, so you can be free of insects — including ticks, black flies and mosquitoes." Burlington Labs? Who are they? Did Bean use their name to lend some kind of credibility? Like I would read the ad and say, "Oh well, Burlington Labs, now then, it's all okay." I felt like I was being schmoozed. Like somehow, they were trying to downplay it, you know, make it sound so not what it is — a chemical shitstorm.

What if instead the ad read: "A chemical shitstorm naturally occurring bug repellent"? The ad writer (I pictured Jon Hamm from *Mad Men* working away at his desk) hoped you'd focus on the words "naturally occurring" to take the edge off. And "synthetic" sounds so benign, right? Not to me. To me, it just seemed like a big fat miss on the double duty register — clothing and bug spray. Who are the people willing to risk wearing clothing like that?

"Stop! Stop trying to solve problems that don't exist!" I shouted at the catalog and held it up so Tom could be offended too.

210

"What are you talking about, babe?" In the kitchen, Tom was busy making dinner and minding his own business. He knows how I savor reading every inch of my Bean catalog, so I'm sure my outburst took him by surprise.

"They want to sell me clothes with a chemical that keeps bugs away. A chemical with God knows what kind of side effects."

From the stove I heard, "No one's making you buy anything, babe."

"They've gone too far this time." I tossed my beloved friend — I mean catalog — on the floor with as much disdain as I could muster.

Tom came out of the kitchen to see what was going on and asked, "Just so I can keep up, is this more upsetting to you than when they came out with clothing that had an SPF rating?"

"More. A lot more, and I don't appreciate the reminder."

"Babe, technology's advancing all the time."

"But some things don't need improvement."

"Shannon, listen to yourself. You're usually interested in new gear, why is this so different?"

"Why can't some things just stay the same?" There was no stopping me now. "Why does everything have to change? My dad hunted in quiet wool pants and coat and was as successful a hunter as anybody nowa-days in scent-blocking camo. What a joke! Gee, let's make clothes for the damn lazy hunter, who shouldn't even be in the woods if he's gonna smoke and eat out, or worse, fill up at the gas station wearing his hunt-ing clothes and then head off into the woods. Geez, it's like cheating in a way. I stop wearing anything perfumed a month before the season opens."

"Babe, you might just be a tiny bit off the rails here. Can I refresh your drink?"

"Am I? I'm tired of performance fabrics. I cringe when I see little kids, toddler age or so" — I held my hand above the floor at knee level—"barely walking, but in Keen shoes. Keen shoes, Tom!"

I left the catalog, and the remnants of my rant, in the living room and headed into the bathroom. I glanced down at my perfume bottle, thought a little more about scent-blocking camo, and looked at myself in the mirror. Tom was right, and I hate it when he's right. I was going nutso over some new product. Where was this all coming from? Hands on the vanity, I leaned in for a closer inspection as if my reflection had the answers, but nothing.

A few minutes later, "Dinner's ready."

I didn't move. Then it hit me. I think I missed seeing the wool clothes. I missed the way things used to be, and then I realized that most of all, I missed my dad. I'd lashed out at my dear friend Bean for moving ahead, turning its back on the past by offering chemical-laced clothing — the future. And it was all because I missed him, the man who wore wool in the woods. The reminders of his era were being replaced by that couple at the farmer's market, and I, I am caught somewhere in between.

"Babe, dinner," again from the kitchen.

I let go of the vanity feeling like I had some sort of answer to my emotional eruption and sat down at the table.

"You okay, bud?" Tom asked gently then put a plate of pork chops with green beans and mashed potatoes in front of me.

"Yeah. I think I miss my dad."

"You know the irony, Shannon? Your dad loved gear. He was always on the lookout for what was new as long as it was quality. I'm not saying bug-juiced clothing is that, but he always researched and found what suited him. Here, put some of this mushroom gravy on your chops, I made a big pan of it."

"Yeah, I know, I know. It just feels like nowadays there's more people like that family we saw at the parade, walking around Scottsdale sporting expensive gear and looking too... perfect."

I put a little extra emphasis on Scottsdale, like it was somehow the bad guy. "How did we go from bread wrappers in our boots to performance wear?"

"I'm not sure, Shannon. It makes you wonder."

That Bastard

"You, ah, got something on your neck," he said and motioned to the left side of my face as we walked back to the picnic table, shotguns in hand.

"Oh…thanks," I said, thinking it was likely dirt from my gun case or whatever and wiped my hand and arm along my neck. I set my gun on the rack, and when I looked at my arm, what I saw made me cringe. White, sticky flakes mixed with sweat. "Ha, it's my new anti-aging cream."

"Your what?" he said, taking the barrel off his gun and putting it away.

"My anti-aging cream. It's so hot out, I must have sweated it all off."

"You know it's not going to work, right? You're aging right now." This from a man whose wrinkles are so deep you could stick a pencil in them and they would hold it.

"I know. But I'm trying to slow down Father Time. That bastard."

"Great, let me know how that works out for ya," he said. Then he hoisted his gun case and ammo box off the picnic table and headed for his car.

I wiped my arm again across my sweaty face and more gunk came off. "Yeah, this is a good look," I muttered. Creamy, expensive anti-aging cream is no match for shooting trap in the desert when it's 110 degrees out. I probably just wiped away $5.00 of the stuff onto my wrist and forearm, which were still pretty taut. So, great job there.

I put Nelli in the back seat, and I sat with the air-conditioning blasting. Then I pulled down the visor and opened the mirror to discover that instead of "helping to reduce the appearance of fine lines and wrinkles" as the ad had promised, the thick, white paste-like cream was trapped in them. My neck looked like a road map to old age. Grimacing, I flipped up the visor and backed up the car. It seemed to be the only thing I could reverse.

I'm not youthful anymore. There, I said it. Almost daily, my body reminds me of that. Some days I look in the mirror and literally cannot believe I am the same person.

I hear the same voice in my head, but who is that person staring back at me? Reflection avoidance has become my new thing.

Well, that, and I've noticed every television commercial showcases a youthful woman dotting anti-aging cream with her ring finger, as if in slow motion, neatly under her eyes. Right…

****

"Focus, Shannon!" I tried to puff the hair distracting me out of my field of view. My ponytail holder can't manage to keep one pesky gray hair corralled. It tickled the top of my right cheek just under my sunglasses and would flutter enough to distract me. "Focus."

It's a constant battle with the wind. I tried hooking it behind my ear, but it managed to flicker just enough to become an annoyance.

"Just pretend it's not there," I said to myself repeatedly as I watched little orange birds zoom across the sky and waited for my turn.

"Pull." The orange bird zoomed across the horizon. A miss. "Damn it."

These few gray hairs had forced me to consider my coloring options. But did I have to do it as I reloaded my gun? Were my teammates thinking about their gray hair right now? Doubtful. I'd never colored mine before and didn't know if I wanted to start. Once you take the plunge into the color vat, you have to keep it up.

Besides the cost, it would be a regular reminder that I'm once again in a battle with Father Time. That bastard.

****

I've either become a leopard or these dark spots on the tops of my hands are age spots making their debut.

"What the hell?" I said out loud, alone in my car stopped at a red light. I looked at my hands on the steering wheel then brought them closer for examination, when *Honk!* Some angry guy behind me with a tatted-up arm flipped me off and yelled for me to "Get a move on!" The light had turned green, and I was still stopped, inspecting my leopard paws.

I looked in the rearview mirror, pushed the accelerator, and flipped him the bird back. "Take that, you bastard!" And wondered where that bit of rage came from.

He zoomed past me. Watching him fly by, I swear I saw long gray hair and a flowing silver beard. Father Time was driving that hopped-up Honda.

****

"Hold still. It's only going to hurt if you keep flinching," Nurse Janet said, trying to numb the area on my neck where the skin tags were growing.

"Why do these things show up?" I asked.

Doctor Kyllo walked into the exam room with scalpel in hand and flippantly said, "You're getting old, kid."

"Really, it's an age thing?" I asked, trying my best to dodge Nurse Janet, who was taking a little too much pleasure with that needle.

"Well, you don't see any young people with them now, do ya?" she said and made the last painful prick with the numbing agent.

"I guess not. Now that you mention it, my dad had some on his neck too."

Snipping away at the tiny bits of flesh, Doctor Kyllo chatted about his last grouse hunting trip. I fidgeted on the exam table and ripped the noisy paper underneath. I squeezed my fists in anticipation of the pain and wondered how come this aging thing happens so fast.

"Okay, that'll do it, kid," he said and slapped my knee.

They left. I sat there for a moment, read the poster about pneumonia, looked at the clear glass jars of cotton balls and tongue depressors, and wondered, *What next?*

******

"Babe, don't worry, you look fine. I love you no matter," Tom said as we got dressed for an evening out.

"Look fine?" I said, looking at him, as if to prove my point, then peered back into the 12x magnification mirror under lights so bright you could perform surgery. I'd started with a 5x mirror but had to amp up the intensity.

"Stop looking in that mirror. We were never intended to see things that close," he teased.

"I can't help it. I need it to put on my eye makeup." And continued to stroke layers of mascara on my lashes, asking myself if they seemed thinner. Tom left the bedroom, and I shouted to him, "I'm still thinking about getting permanent eyeliner.

It's like a tattoo only for your eyes." No response. We'd had that same conversation a million times. I screwed the mascara wand back into its pink tube, tossed it into the drawer, and went out to the kitchen.

"You know, babe, aging is a blessing," he said sweetly.

"I know, it's just that the same makeup on the same face has differ-ent results now, and I hate it. I want my 20-something face back. Heck, I'd even take my 30-something face back."

"Come on, let's go. You're the same beautiful girl I married 25 years ago."

His words faded as he opened the door to the garage and pressed the opener. I turned off the kitchen lights and followed behind.

"Oh my God, 25 years." Maybe it'll be dark wherever we're going.

Vanity aside, I realized that I'm now in a cage match with Father Time. You see, in an unbelievable twist of reality, I started feeling a searing pain in my right index finger. The irony that it's my trigger finger is not lost on me. In the beginning, the pain occurred very infrequently, and only after we moved to Arizona. So I thought maybe I'd done something to it, but I couldn't remember jamming it or catching it on anything. But now it's more frequent. Or "chronic," in medical terms.

"It's the sort of pain that made me yelp out loud," I told my new doctor while I was in for something else. "I can't believe how it just comes on. It's completely random."

"On a scale of one to ten, how bad is the pain?" he asked while manipulating my right hand in all sorts of positions. He examined it, holding it up like maybe he was going to see something on the inside.

"It's a definite 12. It feels like someone's driving a hot, 16-penny nail into the first knuckle joint," I said, adding, "And now the base of my thumb gets it too."

"We'll x-ray it and see what's going on in there." And let go of my hand. Then he told me I could probably get it done right then if I was willing to wait. So I did.

A day or so later, my phone rang. It was the nurse calling to tell me what they found was "just" arthritis.

"Arthritis? Are you kidding me?" I said, stunned.

"Yes, it's quite clear from the x-rays." She sounded confident.

I'm sure she said other things too. Like what to take for the pain, blah, blah, blah.

It didn't matter because I could only think of Father Time with his leather tool belt on, hammer in one hand, 16-penny nail in the other, driving it straight into my trigger finger.

But just for the record, I'm not going to take this lying down. If Father Time wants to mess with me, fine.

"It's go time, baby."

That bastard better be prepared for this gray-haired, anti-aging-creamed, leopard-spotted, arthritic-fingered woman to put up one hell of a fight.

Scorching Texas

"Babe, I'm going back to the car and get us a couple of cold ones. I'll be right back."

Tom's words jarred me out of my near hypnotic state. Still, I continued to stare straight ahead at the vast sky in front of me and only offered a weak, "Great, thanks." I quickly added, "Hurry, I don't want you to miss it."

With that, he was off. I reached over and put my hand on the arm of his chair, making sure it didn't go anywhere. We'd carried the chairs about a 5 iron's distance from the shore to just the right spot. My 5 iron, not Tiger's. So, about 130 yards into the Gulf of Mexico we'd set up our chairs in water up to our armpits and let the warm water rock us back and forth while we waited for sunset.

Our rental car was parked in a tiny unpaved area next to the remote beach. Sanibel's known for many things, but available parking is not one of them. Sea grapes canopied the sandy walk to the secluded beach. The gulf breeze rustled the rounded leaves, which had made me feel I was being cheered on as we made our way through the green tunnel.

Earlier in the day we'd stopped at Walmart and in addition to a foam cooler, ice, and Coors Light, we picked up a couple of cheap, white, molded-plastic chairs. They're perfect for use at the gulf. Not for sitting on the beach, but for sitting in the peaceful water enjoying gentle, almost nonexistent waves, like a giant, soothing bath. We like to sit out at dusk anywhere, but watching the sun go down in the water? Dusk in the gulf? It's almost impossible to be more relaxed.

I sat alone and marinated in the salt water like a turkey the day before Thanksgiving. I poked my fingers up through the water to examine how pruned they'd become.

"Perfect." I was happy to have spent that much time in the water.

Gulf sitting requires exceptional balance. It takes a moment to get your chair situated in a way that allows you to sway but not teeter over backwards, even if it would be in slow motion. Because you're mostly on the back legs of the chair, you rock back and forth, only occasionally coming down with all four legs on the sea bottom.

I watched him disappear into the grapes then turned back around. The only thing between me and Texas was water. A lot of water. Gently moving with the motion of the gulf, I watched the sky show in front of me. The sun made its way down through a few random clouds stacked along the horizon while I waited for Tom to return. For as many sunsets as we've watched, we've never seen the green flash. And when watching in Florida, he and I joke that the exact moment the sun touches the horizon, it's scorching someplace in Texas. I didn't want him to miss that and hoped he was hurrying because we always make the scorching sound together: *kiush*. It's more fun together.

I was alone, relaxed, and enjoying my favorite time of day. The water was calm, the sky however, was changing colors like a…

Huh? What was that? Something brushed against my right ankle.

Yep.

In a split second I was no longer relaxed, no longer enjoying myself, and for the first time realized I wasn't really alone and maybe I was dinner. I popped out of my chair and looked around.

The beach was empty except for a couple who had set up shop about 300 yards away, in an even more private location. Tom was at the car, and I was convinced I was an appetizer for some ravenous sea creature. Was this payback for all the calamari I've eaten?

The water there is so clear you can see 20 feet down, except at sunset, when the surface reflects the shimmery blues of the sky and the orange fireball. All that damned beauty made it impossible for me to see anything below the surface. I tensed up, turned around, and grabbed a chair in each hand. I pulled on them as hard as I could, trying to get out of the water as quickly as possible. But the chairs acted as a drag, and it felt like I wasn't getting anywhere. Part of me didn't want to let them go, thinking they could act as shields, and maybe the whatever-it-was would take a bite out of them instead of me. The other part of me wanted to let them go so I could move faster toward the beach.

With each overly exaggerated step in the waist-deep water, a new vision of terror filled my head. First, the ad for Shark Week on the Discovery Channel, then the movie *Jaws*, which I saw when I was way too young and impressionable. What were my parents thinking letting me see that when I was eleven? Then came *Sharknado*. Don't judge. When you're in crisis, you don't really get to pick and choose what flashes before you. How odd to be thinking about a movie that took Tara Reid from anonymity to semi-anonymity. Worse yet, I was upset that Tara Reid's career trajectory might be my last thought before I was eaten. Crazy, I know.

In the end, I hung on to the chairs. When I finally neared shore, in about a foot of water, I dropped them and hopped out.

Breathing hard, I felt like a survivor. I also felt ridiculous. I stood there looking back out on the water as if whatever had swiped me might burst out of the water and make itself known. But it didn't.

This wasn't Hollywood. Gazing out over the nothingness, I thought, *what if Tom had come back and I was gone?*

I know, I know.

"Hey!" I heard and turned around.

Tom reappeared with a smile on his face and a can in each hand. He walked toward me, saw the cheap chairs lying on their sides, like fish carcasses washed up on shore. Puzzled, he asked, "What are you doing?"

I reached for the cold beer and confessed that I may have freaked out "just a little" when something rubbed against me. That the heebie-jeebies had gotten the better of me, and I couldn't take being out there all by myself.

"I wimped out," I said, not able to look at him. I was covered with goosebumps and shivering. Then I pointed to my ankle as if that would explain everything. As if my leg ended in a shredded, bloody stump.

But in the way Tom always does, he leaned down, gave me a kiss and a reassuring look. "C'mon, babe, nothing's going to get you." He picked up a chair and waded back out into the water. "It was probably just seaweed."

"Uh, okay." But I didn't believe it was seaweed, not for a second. I stood there and wiggled my toes in the sand. The water was serene, disturbed only by his movements. It barely lapped at my feet.

My ankle sensitivity lingered, but just from the ooginess. Still, I looked for some sort of mark, surely there'd be one where the great white grazed me.

"Damn shark."

I imagined a roving gang of teenage sharks who spotted me, then laughing, one of them said to his buddies, "Hey, watch this."

"Smug little fucker," I said and took a swig of cold beer.

"Huh? I can't hear you. What'd you say?" Tom was pretty far out but turned around to look at me. With my free hand I motioned him to keep going.

"Nothing," I said. "Nothing." And I picked up my chair.

The sky was alive now in intense shades of orange, peach, violet, and deeper blues. Scorching Texas was getting close. Tom turned around again, ready to get settled in, and waved at me to join him.

"C'mon," he said, "I don't want you to miss it."

Made in the USA
Middletown, DE
27 April 2021